Winter Time

*Memoirs of a German Sinto
who survived Auschwitz*

Walter Winter, winter 1945.

Winter Time

*Memoirs of a German Sinto
who survived Auschwitz*

WALTER WINTER

TRANSLATED, ANNOTATED AND
WITH A FOREWORD BY

STRUAN ROBERTSON

UNIVERSITY OF HERTFORDSHIRE PRESS

This English edition published in Great Britain in 2004 by
University of Hertfordshire Press
College Lane
Hatfield
Hertfordshire ALIO 9AB

Reprinted 2013

Originally published in German as:
WinterZeit. Erinnerungen eines deutschen Sinto, der Auschwitz überlebt hat
Ergebnisse Verlag, Hamburg, 1999 (ISBN 3-87916-050-3)

English translation by Struan Robertson

British Library Cataloguing in Publication Data
A catalogue record for this book is available from the British Library

ISBN 978-1-902806-38-9 paperback

Design by Geoff Green, Cambridge, CB4 5RA
Cover design by John Robertshaw, Harpenden, AL5 2JB
Printed in Great Britain by MPG Books Group Ltd

TRANSLATOR'S NOTE

The German edition of *WinterZeit* was published in 1999. Walter Winter's memoirs are based on four recorded interviews made on 19 October 1991, 23 June 1992, 8 January 1993 and 23 March 1998. The interviews were then transcribed and edited. The interviews, transcription, editing and accompanying endnotes are attributable to the historians Thomas W. Neumann and Michael Zimmermann.

Contents

List of illustrations

All illustrations are © Walter Winter unless otherwise stated.

Foreword

I was completely unaware of the existence of the Sinti minority in Germany before seeing the Documentation and Cultural Centre of German Sinti and Roma's travelling exhibition documenting the National Socialist genocide of this minority. This unawareness is not unusual even in Germany itself where very few Germans are personally acquainted with Sinti and Roma but where prejudice and discrimination against 'Zigeuner' are rife. Prior to this I had also understood the Holocaust to have been exclusively the Nazi extermination of the Jews. This is a common misconception.

I first met Walter Winter in connection with bringing this Holocaust exhibition to Hamburg. I took along my copy of his book for him to sign and he informed me that Professor Ian Hancock, director of the Texas Romani Archives and Documentation Center, had proposed that the book be translated into English when they had met at the Stockholm International Forum on the Holocaust in January 2000. I agreed that his remarkable story should be made available to a wider readership. Thereafter we met regularly in his cosy apartment or on his sunny balcony to co-operate on this English edition of his book. Listening to his personal story I became aware of what it has meant for him to be both a German national and a member of a minority, being regarded as an outsider in his own country. Confronted with prejudice and discrimination as a schoolchild, Walter Winter learnt the necessity of "being better than the others". This attitude epitomises his life. It is perhaps his experience of living in two worlds, being both an outsider and a German, that has formed his strength of personality.

Winter Time is a first-hand account of the German Sinti Holocaust. Walter Winter presents his experiences of concentration-camp life with a down-to-earth, take-life-as-it-comes attitude. His deportation to Auschwitz-Birkenau was a momentous event in his life but he recounts it as though it were an everyday occurrence like any other. This unsettling and provocative viewpoint negates both the idea of fate and our conventional view of the victim.

Having survived the Holocaust and the war Walter Winter returned to his homeland Germany and spent his working years building a business and raising a family. Retirement has granted him the time to become engaged in commemorative work. He is convinced that it is only by confronting the past that we can understand the present and secure the future. His book and educational work in schools and other venues are his personal contribution to the fight against racism and intolerance.

On 19 November 2003, almost sixty years after the elimination of the 'Gypsy Camp' in Auschwitz-Birkenau, Walter Winter, as a member of a delegation of Sinti and Roma Holocaust survivors led by Romani Rose, chairman of the Central Council of German Sinti and Roma, travelled to Berlin to meet with Dr Christina Weiss, Minister of Culture, to protest against the decision to use the pejorative and undifferentiated term 'Zigeuner' in the inscription on the proposed Sinti and Roma Holocaust Memorial and to argue that the following quotation from former German President Roman Herzog be inscribed:

> Der Völkermord an den Sinti und Roma ist aus dem gleichen Motiv des Rassenwahns, mit dem gleichen Vorsatz, mit dem gleichen Willen zur planmäßigen und endgültigen Vernichtung durchgeführt worden wie der an den Juden. Sie wurden

im ganzen Einflussbereich der Nationalsozialisten systematisch und familienweise vom Kleinkind bis zum Greis ermordet.

"The Nazi genocide of the Sinti and Roma, like that of the Jews, was racially motivated and implemented with the intention and resolve to systematically and definitively exterminate these peoples. The Sinti and Roma were systematically murdered, indiscriminately from babies to the elderly, throughout German occupied territory."

The term 'Zigeuner' is the stigmatising word used over centuries by the majority populations in German-speaking lands and by the National Socialists to describe these minorities. Within the German-speaking sphere, the terms Sinti and Roma are used by these two discriminate minorities to name themselves. The English name Romany is the equivalent generic non-discriminatory term used to describe these peoples. It is indicative of the post-war treatment of German Sinti and Roma that eighty-four-year-old Walter Winter was compelled to make such a journey to argue such a case.

STRUAN ROBERTSON

dedicated to my wife
Marion
(W. S. W.)

PART ONE

The years 1919–1943

Family

We were nine children: Erich, Emma, Rosa, me, Maria, Hermann, Bernadine, Heinrich and Adolf. The last three of us nine children were late arrivals. When our parents were travelling by bicycle or with a horse-drawn wagon the elder siblings had to take care of the younger ones. My brother Erich, six years older than me, had to cook for us. He watched over us until our parents returned. He was very strict with us. It was like this: we children mucked in, whether it was the youngest aged only five or six, or the eldest, this was second nature to us. When the elder siblings had something to do we gave a hand where we could.

Much earlier, before I started school, we lived in Wittmund in East Frisia. My father had a small cottage there. My father and my mother travelled around by bicycle peddling clothing and fabrics. They had a large suitcase on the back, they travelled with this. As at that time we also had horses, my father was good with animals. He was good with cattle; he was good with horses. He also traded horses, he had done everything imaginable. Our immediate neighbour was a Jew, a horse slaughterer. His name was Cohn. On the corner lived a horse trader with whom my father often had dealings. He wanted my father to work for him; he wanted my father to visit horse fairs on his behalf. But my father did not want to do this, he wanted to remain independent.

We lived in Wittmund for a long time, until 1927. On the whole this period was not bad. Our neighbours opposite

Walter Winter's father Johann Winter, between the age of 40 and 50.

were carpenters. It was customary in East Frisia for neighbours to visit one another. But the horse slaughterer Cohn was taboo. He personally was not taboo but his profession was. Our customs prohibit us from associating with horse slaughterers.[1] We liked to talk to him, as an acquaintance and neighbour he was very nice.

My parents' family had been artistes and showmen or travelling entertainers as they were once called. Sadly, the relevant documents were taken from us during the Nazi period

4

Walter Winter's mother.

and they cannot be procured again. My father grew up in a caravan. One day he said, "Man! I have the itch to be travelling again." To the rear of us, a few houses further on, lived a cartwright. My father bargained with him, "If you build me a caravan and a wagon you can have my land and house." And so we had a caravan and a wagon again. My old man, my father, had horses anyway. Then he set off, in 1927. When there was a horse fair in Lingen on the river Ems, in Leer, or in Aurich, we would visit it.

In those days there were separate campsites for Gypsies.

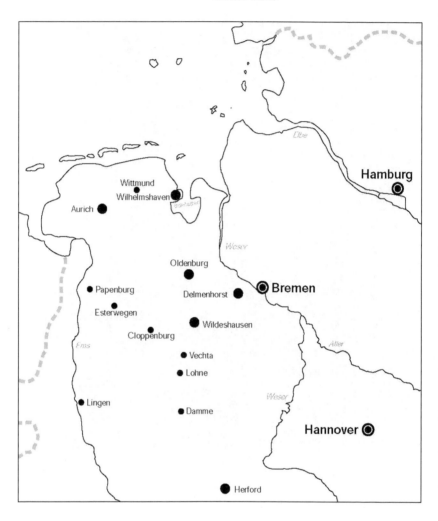

Map of north-west Germany showing the places relevant to Walter Winter's biography.

You were not allowed to stop anywhere else; they took you to these campsites. These sites were on the whole in good order. But there were no toilets, no mains water supply. You had to fetch the water from the pump or well. In the past, others had to do the same. Such campsites were generally outside a village or town, quite a distance outside. We boys were always

Walter Winter's grandmother at the rear of her house in Cloppenburg, 1933.

happy when there were other caravans there. We could then get into conversation, play together, play skittles or go fishing.

When I go on holiday abroad now, in Spain or Italy or Sri Lanka, I still find a sense of family there, like with the Turks[2]

Members of the family, with relatives, in Cloppenburg, in the early 1930s. Brother Erich is in his football gear, kneeling.

here. In the past that was also true of us. When someone was your cousin, then he was your cousin. The essential thing was that you respected him. He was simply your cousin. It was just so. No one was allowed to say anything against him; no one could run him down. No one was permitted to say anything against the family.

We were often on the move but, in between times, we visited my grandparents in Cloppenburg. We visited them whenever we had a few days free. Later we had a car which was better still. On the days between the funfairs and festivals my parents often said, "You know what? Today we'll drive over to Cloppenburg. There we'll all be together." Or to Oldenburg, where we had recently lived. Such distances were not great, East Frisia, South-Oldenburg to Herford in Westphalia. Then back again. Sometimes we travelled together with our nearest relatives, with my grandparents or one of my father's brothers. Sometimes we met up on our travels and several caravans stood together for a night or two before parting again. They simply had to see one another again. Then we really celebrated, with music and dancing. Afterwards everything was fine again.

During the winter we were at home. We set out again at Easter when the weather was better. We built a shed specially into which the caravan fitted. At this time we still had horses. We had a stall for the horses at the rear. We also had hay meadows so that the horses had feed for the winter. We planted potatoes, cabbage and vegetables; we had everything at home. We ploughed our land ourselves with the horses, despite it being marshland. We then attached float-like wooden 'shoes' to the horses' hooves to prevent them sinking into the marsh. My father turned over the soil. We children lent a hand at potato harvest, hay harvest, twice a year. Hay harvest meant one or two weeks' haymaking. At that time the grass had to be scythed and then turned over with the pitchfork. A week would fly by.

School

When I started school in 1926 we still lived in Wittmund. My parents returned to travelling in 1927. At this time my father owned land in Oldenburg. We built a wooden house there. Then I went to school in Oldenburg. I must say that I was lucky to find a very good teacher there, the headmaster Mr Cordes. My schoolmistress was Miss Hillmann, also a very good, kind teacher. I spent three good compulsory years at school in Oldenburg. At that time in Oldenburg, children of school age were not allowed to travel. That was why three of us had to remain at home; we were of school age. We had to walk four kilometres to school each morning, winter and summer. In winter we were out in the morning whilst it was still dark, sometimes returning home in the dark.

These three years of school were decisive for me. I skipped two years and moved up from the third to the fifth year. Headmaster Cordes' son was in the same class as me. We got along well with each other. We played football together.

My parents travelled, returning to us twice during the week. Friends from my mother's side of the family, a man and a woman, kept an eye on us, cooking and looking after us. When we returned from school my sisters or I had to feed the horses. Sometimes I arrived back a little later, having played football with my friends on the way, they were *real* friends!

In the three years that we children remained at home we owned 120 chickens, ducks, guinea fowl and geese. We also had forty-five pigeons. Each day I took a basket of eggs to a shopkeeper, roughly a two-kilometre walk, and bartered them for provisions. The shopkeeper was happy to receive the eggs and we did not need money for provisions.

When these three years of school were over new regulations came into force. Children of school age were allowed to accompany their parents on their travels once again – on condition that they were entered, as being of school age, in their parents' peddlers' licence. My father did this.

Headmaster Cordes spoke to my father. "Mr Winter, leave the boy here, he has ability, grasps things well. He can attend secondary school together with my son. You don't need to pay anything; he can live and board with us. He can share my son's room."

I was particularly good at drawing with pencil or quill and Mr Cordes thought I could become an architect. But naturally I wished to leave and tugged the back of my father's jacket.

"Well," my father said, "I will have a word with my son."

But, once we had left, we had left. This was probably the biggest mistake I have ever made. What did I know then? I had never been away from home and my father decided, "I won't allow this, I don't want this." And so I accompanied him.

After that we attended school on our travels. And the older you became, the more you became conscious of, the more you realised that, even as children we were discriminated against. When as a child you had barely learnt to walk and started to play with other children, adults or even children themselves called out, "Gypsy! Gypsy!" At that age children do not know what they are saying. This insult had been learnt in the parental home, from the parents.

It was the same at school. A whisper went round the class every time we attended school while on our travels. We arrived with others; we were nine brothers and sisters. Also the children of the family with whom we travelled together came with us. From time to time we were twelve children who all went to school together.

In the past children from the first to the fourth or fifth class sat together in the same classroom. When we arrived the whispering would begin, "Gypsies! Gypsies!"

Some teachers asked each of us in turn, "Which class are you in? And which class are you in?" We were then placed with the children of the same age group. Other teachers did not do this. They moved the local children, sitting in the first row, to the back, sat us all in the emptied first row and asked us, "How far did you get in your last school?"

We opened the exercise books. "Up to here."

"Right, carry on from there!" That was all. The teacher no longer concerned himself with us.

In the breaks we were made fun of in the school playground. Of course, not by all the children. There were also those who asked, "Don't you have anything to eat?"

"No."

"Come here, you can have some of mine."

But there were always those who taunted us with, "Gypsy, Gypsy Joker, Hit you with a poker." It depended on whom we got as a teacher. We saw how they treated us during lessons. We kept a low profile. We said to ourselves, "Wait until lessons are over, then we'll take revenge." Well, what else could we do?

When school was over for the day we got those who had taunted us. This was the only way we could defend ourselves. They got a good beating! The next day they sneaked on us to the teacher. Then, naturally, we received a good hiding on the backside. In those days corporal punishment was permitted, either on the hand or on the backside. But we had to defend ourselves. We could never go anywhere alone or in twos, we had to go about in groups to defend ourselves. Even as a child this was so.

But, generally, the people in the country were not so unfriendly. When we were camped in the yard of an inn and left for school in the morning, sometimes we had no lunch because we had overslept or were in a hurry. Then, my mother gave us twenty Pfennig.

"Go to the baker and buy some cake."

So, we went to the baker or to a farmer and said, "We are at school and have nothing to eat, could you give us some buttered bread?"

"Yes, of course."

We often did this. Some refused and chased us from their doors.

During the time we were travelling I left school, unfortunately without a school-leaving certificate. I was fourteen years old; for me school was over.

Police

The local police were on horseback or on bicycles. There were real swine among them, real swine. There was a week between funfairs and *Schützenfeste*.[3] We travelled in horse-drawn caravans. We camped together for a night at an inn, for example. We fed the horses, slept and continued the next day. Then the police arrived by bicycle or on horseback.

"Harness the horses, immediately, immediately! Leave!" They 'transported' us, that is to say they escorted us as far as the next district. The boundaries to villages, towns and districts were clearly marked. They took us to one of these boundaries. There we were met by the police officer from the next district. We were not even allowed to feed the horses en route, not to halt, nothing. We were handed over at the next district.

But we had to feed the horses at some time or halt over night. Then it was, "Well, you can halt for twenty-four hours." And on again the next day. People talk about the good old days. When I hear that! You did not realise this as a child but when I think about this today I must, in all honesty, say they were dreadful times.

When four or five caravans stood together, you knew for certain that the police would soon arrive. You were so careful not to attract attention. Either you asked at an inn, "May we stay for one or two days? We'll pay. We'll stand a round. We'll come in and drink something too."

Most landlords allowed this. "Yes, of course, naturally." We stabled the horses.

But the police appeared anyway and asked, "Do you have authorisation?"

"Yes."

"From whom?"

"From the landlord."

They then went to the inn and browbeat the landlord as to why he had allowed Gypsies to stay.

Some landlords were resolute. "This is my property and I'll do what I like."

We spent money. In those days, a beer cost a Groschen and spirits five Pfennig. When several caravans came together we celebrated and the landlord made good money. We took care that nothing untoward happened, that everything was in order, that nothing was stolen. It was immediately stipulated that no one do anything wrong.

There were places where we were liked. We met up with others at Whitsun, Easter or other holidays. Some landlords even said, "You can take hay from the loft for the horses." I cannot say whether they did that out of solidarity or for business reasons but there was no compulsion to do this had they not wanted to. These were friends who were on Christian-name terms with my father, who were always happy to see him.

Other landlords were fearful and said, "Mr Winter, could you continue on your way early tomorrow? Otherwise, I will have problems with the police." Then we continued on our way.

My father was convivial, he would buy a round of drinks when we were sitting in a tavern and there were three or four men at the bar. Then he'd say, "Fill their glasses." He was popular everywhere. I think I am also popular here among the fairground people. But today I am a different person. What I have been through has made me distrustful. Totally distrusting. In the past I was not so. But over the past years, now that I am more settled and have time to reflect, I have become so.

Football

I have played football ever since I was a schoolchild. When we took up our winter quarters in Oldenburg we camped in the district of Osternburg. The glassworks' football club, Frisia, was right next door to us. The fence of the sports ground adjoined the coal merchant's where we stayed. My brother joined the club. He trained with them and played for them when he was only sixteen. The glassworks was closed down and the Frisia club was taken over by VfL Oldenburg. We continued playing there. I was ten or eleven years old and played for the boys' team. My brother Erich played in the league; at the age of seventeen or eighteen he was a coveted footballer. We did not realise this at the time, we simply saw how people yelled and went crazy when he got the ball.

I passed through Osternburg on the way home from school and played in a street team with the boys I knew there. They waited for me, they were already there. We left our satchels beneath a tree and played between the oak trees. On a winter evening it was four or half past four, almost dark, when we arrived home. Our shoes were ruined. I received an immediate dressing down by my mother but it had been fun and you realised you had skill. You could control the ball. It then became more interesting.

It was the same for my brother. The matches he played then! My goodness! Important matches for the North German team and three international matches. Erich was known by the public as 'Blackie'. We were known to be Gypsies but as sportsmen we were popular.

At this time, in 1933, Hitler came to power. Two brothers who were members of the SS played in the VfL Oldenburg first team. They knew we were Gypsies but they told Erich, "So long as we are here, nothing will happen to you." Well, then came the war and we were booted out of the club anyway. There was also a Jew, a first-rate goalkeeper. He had already left by 1936.

Erich was an outstanding player, a feared centre forward. He had a style like the future Rudi Völler. Even at this time he received money from the club, not much but his hotel was paid for when the team played away and the club paid for his kit. And they collected him when we were travelling. They arrived by car and picked him up. He was a fantastic footballer. When he was forward with the ball he was unstoppable. The other local clubs, Leer, Aurich, Oldenburg, Bremen, St Pauli – at this time HSV (Hamburg) had not entered the picture – all wanted him. But my father said, "No, my boy, you remain here."

One match I will never forget, against St Pauli at Easter. At that time we were living four kilometres outside Oldenburg. Erich's bicycle was in need of repair. We had to repair it before we could leave. Strictly speaking, they should have kicked off but they pleaded with the referee so that he waited. In the clubroom three men dressed my brother. He didn't enter the field round the front but jumped over the railing at the rear. When the spectators saw him they clapped and yelled, "There he is! There's Pummel!" This was a lazy pronunciation of his Sinti name, Pumpel. It is usual for Sinti to have, in addition to their official first name, a Sinti first name which we use among ourselves. My Sinti name is Fiso. Erich was a great player, he played in three internationals. He was very popular in the club. When the Nazis kicked us out of the club the players shook their heads in disbelief. They didn't know what to say. Some said, "Man, that can't be true!"

Showman

In 1934, my parents said, and I can hear them to this day, "We can't continue like this. This Hitler ... We must blend in with the people." We gave the horses away, we began as fairground show people and opened a shooting gallery. We stuck to this and it became part of my growing up.

At the age of fourteen I drove the towing vehicle. That was a vehicle without a tailboard. When this was a car the bodywork behind the driving seat had to be cut away. We bought our first car for 300 Mark in Leer, in East Frisia. It was a Protos. The make no longer exists. It was a cabriolet, with a hood. It seated seven. We hitched two wagons to it, a trailer and a caravan. A driving licence was not required for a towing vehicle. Nevertheless, my brother acquired one, he was over eighteen years of age.

At first, we had a struggle at *Schützenfeste*, funfairs and markets. Some fairground people were very nice but we were always called "Gypsies". Usually we were the only Sinti[4] among the fairground people. In Cloppenburg there were others who had switched profession but that was some years later. When, during the Hitler period, several Sinti families came together we were immediately conspicuous.

In these years we made friends with the young fairground people. They were genuine friends. When today people greet you with, "Well, my friend, how are you?" that is no genuine friendship. When, a few years ago, a colleague greeted me with, "Hello, how are you, my friend?" I answered, "You're

Erich with the Winter family's shooting gallery at a funfair, 1934.

not my friend. You're a colleague."

"What do you mean?"

"Friends are rare, very rare. You are perhaps a close acquaintance, a colleague."

Friends are not easy to find. I had a friend in the navy who was drowned. He was a true friend. I think you must be able to be completely candid with a friend. I must be able to confide in another without this confidence being broken. But when someone greets you with, "So, my friend, how are you?" that isn't to be taken seriously.

We soon had our regular *Schützenfeste*. My father was some-one who got on well with people. Now and again at these funfairs he stood a barrel of beer. People liked him a lot. As a boy I was always happy when these funfairs in July and August were over. When it approached midnight at one of these funfairs the drunken country louts, I have to say this, were insufferably vulgar. They made lewd remarks to our girls. Then we boys left the shooting gallery and often gave them a good beating.

The first car owned by the Winter family, a Protos, Jever, 1934, Walter Winter is in the middle wearing a cap, his father and second youngest brother are left; his mother and youngest sister are behind in the caravan. The others are relatives.

Later in the year the markets began, cattle markets and horse fairs, with shooting galleries and carousels. It began with the Vechta stubble market, Vechta is in Oldenburg. Then came Oldenburg, Bremen and elsewhere. *Schützenvereine* also welcomed us. When it came to assigning places at funfairs and the other booth owners saw that we were to be in the same row as them, they wanted to be positioned elsewhere. Our booth was fourteen metres long and full of goods. Five of us operated the booth, my three sisters, my brother and I. We had target shooting, bottle shooting, flower shooting and shooting at soft toys. I was responsible for target shooting but sometimes for flower shooting or bottle shooting.

In autumn 1934, because the trailer had become ever heavier, we bought a larger car as towing vehicle, a Cadillac, only two years old. It was a wonderful car. Grafen von Galen from Münster had owned it.[5] We exchanged it for our old car and in addition my father's gold watch and a repeater with chimes, and cash. It was so large that it was actually possible to

Walter Winter, second from the right, together with two sisters, a cousin and friends, in front of the caravan.

In 1934, the Winter family bought a Cadillac from the Earl of Galen in Münster. Walter's brother Erich is standing left with an uncle seated in the car.

sleep in it, which was just as well as my parents travelled with nine children. It was a Pullman limousine, very beautiful, with running-board lights and a built-in compressor in case of a puncture.

At the beginning of the war everyone had to deliver up their cars when they were of a particular year of production. Our car came within this category. We received the current value of the car. With this money we bought a lorry, a Hansa-Lloyd. It was built in Bremen. Before I was conscripted into the navy, in December 1939, I drove this lorry for three months to and from the airport in Cloppenburg. I had to be there at seven in the morning. In the evenings we could drive as long as we wished. That meant we could work overtime. I notched up many hours. I deposited the money in an account at the bank. We worked on enlarging the airport; all my relatives worked there, had to work there.[6] They sat in the back of the lorry while I drove them to the airport. After I was conscripted the lorry stood unused. Later my father had to hand it in. He kept the shooting gallery. But *Schützenfeste* were not held during the war.

At the end of August 1939 we were down in Emsland, in Papenburg. We had not set up the shooting gallery when mobilisation began. We packed everything and travelled to Cloppenburg.

The Nazi Period

After 1933 we behaved as my father told us to: "Don't attract attention, behave correctly, do not provoke anyone! You see how it is." We heeded our parents. We kept a low profile. The situation became very bad. When you entered a town you had the feeling of being observed and looked at strangely by people. We were dressed no differently from others, but we were dark skinned. You could really sense the looks boring into our backs. When people passed by on the other side of the road, then … the look alone, when they stared across. Today we would probably no longer attract attention. But in those days there were very few people of dark appearance. When people saw a person of dark appearance they immediately saw a Gypsy.

At this time there were always people at *Schützenfeste* who were anti-Gypsy. And I was dark. My father always told us, even as children, "Don't speak our language, speak German, so they won't have anything against us. Don't speak Romani anywhere!"[7] Before the Nazi period people were not so anti-Gypsy. You could go to a farmer with a milk can, a five-litre can for we were a large family.

My mother would say, "Son, go, here is fifty Pfennig, ask them to fill it." Occasionally farmers poured in milk without taking any money. They would say, "Take care not to spill any."

We also received hay for the horses. That was from 1927 to 1930. But when Hitler became more popular, at the beginning of the 1930s, people were suddenly different.

Once I got a slap round the face. I was still attending school at the time. The SA marched through Osternburg, flag up front. Everyone standing at the roadside had to raise their arms in salute. I naturally didn't do this but, wanting to see these apes, was standing at the front. One of the SA marching directly behind the flag saw this. He left the line, came toward me and slapped me round the face. The bastard knocked me sideways.

"Can't you raise your arm?"

That was my last parade.

In Osternburg the SA screamed at many people during these parades. Before 1933 Osternburg was totally communist – particularly the workers at the glassworks. My brother was a member of their boxing club – one hundred per cent communist. During the war, when as a sailor I returned on leave, I was surprised how this communist district had shifted allegiance. Almost all had become Nazis.

My sisters liked to go dancing and enjoy themselves now and again but this was almost impossible under the Nazis. When we wanted to go dancing, for safety's sake, we all had to go together. When you danced with a local girl the immediate reaction was, "Look, the Gypsy there, he's making out with one of our girls!" When we heard this we quickly came together: "You know what, we had better leave. There's nothing here for us!"

At this time our grandparents lived in Cloppenburg. Once we attended a dance there, my youngest aunt, and some of us siblings and cousins. We did not know that SA and SS from Esterwegen would be coming. There was a concentration camp in Esterwegen.[8]

We danced. All of a sudden, we heard, "Dance contest!" We participated but so did many SA and SS. That wasn't to our liking.

I said to my cousin, standing next to me, "Look, an SA man has won first prize!"

Although I spoke quietly one of them must have over-

Walter Winter is on the left with brother Erich second from the right, around 1934.

heard me. They came to me and claimed that I had said, "Strange, that an SA man won the first prize!" I left as they all wanted to get me. I was gone, running. They chased me. I was naturally a bit faster as they were in uniform. Finally, I ran into a public house and hid in the toilet. They caught me there. There was an SS man among them who lived in the same tenement house as my grandmother. He was my age, you could almost say we grew up together. He had also been at the dance, had seen everything and had given chase. He had a higher rank than the other SA and SS men who were chasing me. He blew his whistle and they halted and came to him. He said to me, "Beat it!" That was my salvation. Had he not been there they would have done for me. It was terrible; soon we didn't go anywhere any more.

After this the situation became even worse. We were in Oldenburg at the *Krämermarkt*.[9] We were members of the Association of Fairground Workers. The people in the Association treated my father as one of them. They liked him also because, at this time, we still owned a good car and business, which they respected. We all wore the same attire at the shooting gallery and earned our living this way. The general meeting of the Association of Fairground Workers took place in Oldenburg. They had a sign: 'Jews and Gypsies – No entry!' My father entered anyway because his colleagues took him with them, but a man named Aalhorn from Oldenburg stood at the executive table in SA uniform. Previously he had been pleased when my father had stood him a drink. Now my father had to leave.

In Oldenburg there lived a wholesaler by the name of Hirschberg. In 1936 he said to my father while I was present, "Jan." (My father's name was Johann but they were on familiar terms.) "Jan, we plan to emigrate, do you want to come with us? My son is already in America, he is preparing everything. I will follow him."

My father answered, "How can I manage that with nine children? I don't have the money."

"You don't need money. I'll take care of that, and we'll make a new start there."

My father said, "But I don't speak English. How would I survive?"

In all events my father left it at that. Had he known what

was to occur and had he read Hitler's book *Mein Kampf*, perhaps, he would have reacted differently.

When the war began, for the first time my father camped in my grandparents' yard in Cloppenburg. Here we were all together, my uncles with their families and my grandparents. Everyone said, "It's starting, everyone will be called up." My father moved out of the yard. One of my uncles lived in a hut in a large sandpit, adjacent to woodland, on the edge of the town. My father parked his caravan next to this hut. Later, during the time Erich and I were in the Wehrmacht, all Sinti who had previously been camped on private sites in Cloppenburg had to move to this sandpit. They were ordered here, they had to report regularly to the police, they were not allowed to leave the town.[10] It made no difference that Erich and I, as well as several cousins and uncles, were in the Wehrmacht. An uncle was killed and a close acquaintance was killed, also a Sinto, a nice boy, we grew up together. Altogether, from Cloppenburg, five or six Sinti were killed in the war.

Labour Service and Navy

During 1938–9 I had to do Labour Service (RAD).[11] After three months all the young men, except me, were promoted. At that time I didn't give it much thought as I wasn't very interested in promotion. But shortly before discharge I heard that there had been a official communication: I was a Gypsy and therefore could not receive promotion.

In Labour Service 1938. Walter Winter is on the right.

Walter Winter, in the navy 1941–42.

My Labour Service came to an end at the start of the war. My brother was the first to receive his enlistment orders. He was to join the air force. Then I got mine: to report to the navy on 1 January 1940. I remained in the navy until March 1942. I was stationed in Wilhelmshaven where I received four special trainings. According to my officers, I was an exemplary sailor. We Sinti were motivated. "Be inconspicuous! Always be, when possible, better than the others!" So that they could not call us "asocial!" or "lazy!" This ambition was second nature, "You must be better than the others," so as not to stand out. I played football and handball in the navy. We made sports trips from the base. It was called 'publicity'. We travelled all around, to Cologne, Hamburg, Dortmund, Wuppertal. I had to play football and then handball or conversely first handball then football. As substitute I was back and forth between the two sports. We travelled with twenty-eight men, two officers, the others almost all petty officers. We had three national players in our football team. Why the publicity? I never gave it a thought. I must say that at this time I was solely a sportsman. Nothing else interested me. I was a popular sportsman, in the company and in the navy. I was involved with everything that had to do with sport, volleyball, netball, handball, football.

After the war I never saw any of the chaps I was with in the navy. Seven were drowned when their warship came under fire as it passed through the English Channel. Three survived. Idiot that I was, I repeatedly tried to leave Wilhelmshaven. That's how it is ... when you are young. I thought, "Hell! The others get to leave. Transferred. Transferred. And you remain stuck here." And then the chaps who had been posted returned. Man! As though they were returning from a holiday of glorious weather and sunshine! But my sports officer wouldn't let me out of his clutches. I regularly added my name to the lists when chaps were to be posted to Sicily or the German-occupied Mediterranean islands. But he got hold of the lists and crossed me off. Each time he yelled at me, "Are you crazy? I forbid you. That's the last time you do that!"

Finally I managed to get posted. My sports officer was on three weeks' leave. During this time there was a list, "So many men to Helgoland!" My name stood at the top of the list. Then he returned from leave. Oh, did he bawl me out! Two days later, in Helgoland, I had to pack, having been posted

The Wilhelmshaven navy football team with Walter Winter, third from the right.

back to Wilhelmshaven. He was a leading seaman but we were on first-name terms, when we were alone. Of course, we couldn't do this when officers were present. I was the only one who played volleyball with the officers. He would call me when they were short of an officer, even when I was on duty, "Walter, come immediately! We're a man short." Then I had to drop everything. I had to hop on the tram up to the sports hall. Sport was my life. I played every team game imaginable.

I was gun captain of a four-barrelled anti-aircraft battery. During one air raid on Wilhelmshaven I was manning the gun. My left hand fired a single barrel for drawing a line on the target, the right hand the four-barrelled battery. An aeroplane, one of those huge Wellington bombers, appeared in the moonlight. It was low, perhaps seven or eight hundred metres. Clearly visible. I fired the single barrel, intentionally too low. Then, the leading seaman standing behind me with the sights shouted, "Higher, higher, higher!" It was a rotating gun. I had the pilot directly in my sights, I could have downed him with two shots. I fired above and below him. The third time the leading seaman ordered, "Battery fire!" He was standing behind me with my seat between his legs with a sight on the plane. Then I had to obey, I couldn't refuse. I gave continuous fire and you could clearly see, how he ... up front in the cockpit. The bomber shook like a leaf. I thought, "So, you've hit the target. Now, they're out of the game." A propeller ceased to rotate. The plane dropped one hundred metres then straightened out again. Man, that was a hell of a shock! Then it was out of range. The next thing I heard through my earphones was that it had come down a kilometre away, on the shore at Jadebusen. I thought, "God, damn it." I couldn't counter his order. Afterwards he gave me a good ticking-off but I couldn't stand him anyway. I almost hit him. I was awarded a pennant for my hit, for our gun crew.

I was allowed to be gun captain of a four-barrelled anti-aircraft battery. But there was always someone watching me, who had me under surveillance. It was one of my own roommates but it took me a long time to realise this. I said, "Man, you're always here. Why don't you go out! Don't you ever want to go ashore?"

"No", he said, "I'm not interested." I was literally under guard. I had freedom of movement but I was never alone.

Discharge[12]

Then it was March 1942. All the young men who had been conscripted with me were promoted to petty officers. I was the only one not to be promoted, just as in Labour Service. I had a friend in the orderly room. I went to him.

"Look here, what's going on? Something isn't right!"

"Yes, but I'm not allowed to tell you."

I begged him and he answered, "All right, but in confidence. You are classified as 'non-Aryan'. I have your promotion here on my desk but I am not allowed to grant it and I'm not allowed to tell you."

I went straight to my leading seaman, "Look here!" I confronted him with the situation.

"What do you want, I know nothing about this," he replied.

"Oh yes! That's how it is. I have it from a totally reliable source. I want to see the naval officer."

I got to talk to the naval officer. I told him plainly, "I'm not prepared to serve in the navy as a mere stopgap, although I'm ready to defend my parents and brothers and sisters at home. I'm German but under these conditions, as fair game, I don't see any reason to fight."

He was sympathetic. "What's written here is out of the question! That's just not on! 'Non-Aryan'. Such a good seaman and we must lose you. Anyhow, for now you remain here! I'll look into it."

He took my documents to the Commander-in-Chief of

the Fleet. That was Rear Admiral Dönitz.[13]

Dönitz sent the documents to Berlin, to the Reich Security Main Office.[14] My papers were excellent. The process took six months, during which time I remained in the navy. Then the documents were returned. I could remain, if I wished, with the proviso that I had no right of rank or promotion. I had duties with no rights. I considered the situation. In Wilhelmshaven we had had a number of air raids, death being a hair's breadth away, my life being on a razor's edge. I thought: die here, for what? Without acknowledgement, without rights? No, I would prefer to be discharged.

I said to my sports officer, "Why should I remain here and fight? For whom?"

"I can't blame you for thinking that. But, good heavens, what will happen to our sports club?"

"Look for another sportsman."

"Yes, but who?" He knew I was a Sinto. He shook his head, "How is such a thing possible? They send our best men packing." I had completed four training courses. I was a specialist. It was so ... You can't alter the fact that you are born a Sinto. You are a human being. No individual should be discriminated against because of skin colour, race, religion or belief. But that's Utopian!

When I left my sports officer was standing above on the bridge. He stood there waving me goodbye until I disappeared from his sight. Willi, that was his first name, came from Wuppertal.

Arrest

I returned to Oldenburg. My service papers contained the entry: 'N.z.v. – unsuitable material.' I had to surrender my service papers at the military authority in Oldenburg.

The officer sitting there looked at my service papers and said, "No, things don't work so easily. You don't get home that easily. One moment. Take a seat in the next room."

I sat down. He made a phone call then came to me, head bowed. "Mr Winter, you are discharged. I don't understand."

I was out of the Wehrmacht.

Then I filed an application for discharge for my brother. He was at the Russian front. The Wehrmacht had probably already started its own proceedings. Four weeks later my brother returned. We went home together and a few days later we were assigned compulsory work. My brother Erich, my sister Maria and I worked at the airport in Damme, near Vechta. We had a lorry and I was employed by the Vechta motor pool working for a large flagstone works. We also got hold of a car and my brother cut out the back and used it as a loading platform.

I was unable to load the slabs alone. I went to the woman owner – her husband was fighting in the war. I said, "I can't manage alone, I need a mate."

"Alright, go to the boiler room and choose someone there. Take him with you." And who was it who became my mate? Georges Pompidou, who was later to become President of France.[15] But, of course, I wasn't to know that at the time. He

was a French officer, a prisoner-of-war. During the day he
had freedom of movement, in the evening he had to return to
the POW camp. He spoke a little broken German. We got on
well together.

I said to him, "Give me your word that you won't do a
runner. They will imprison me if you do." I told him how I
had been discharged from the navy.

Later I adapted a vehicle as my brother had done. We were
employed as drivers for the Vechta district council: my brother
for Vechta, me for Damme, for the Post Office, public houses,
undertakers, whatever came up.

Every Saturday I met up with my brother Erich and my
sister Maria in Vechta, where they had a room. I arrived from
Damme either by train or by car. I would leave the car in
Vechta and we would travel home together. It was now the
beginning of March 1943. I was waiting at Vechta station. We
wanted to take a particular train home but my brother and
sister were not there.

"Man, where are they?" I waited a half hour and then
drove to their flat.

The landlady came out with her head hanging low. "Mr
Winter, I have something to tell you. They took your brother
and sister away."

"Who took them away?"

"The police." Then it dawned on me. There had been
rumours about such arrests.

"Heavens, what do I do now?" I thought as I parked the
car, "You can't travel during the day, you can't risk it, they'll
be waiting at the station and will nab you." I waited until the
evening and quickly bought a rail ticket. I didn't board the
train from the platform but from the other side. I travelled
home where my parents were waiting for us. I told them
what had happened. I stayed at home for three days. My
brother and sister were gone and we had no idea where.

On the third day I said to my father, "You know what! I'll
travel to Damme and collect the lorry. Then at least you will

have a lorry here, so that you'll be mobile."

My father answered, "I'll give you money, you disappear. Anywhere. The main thing is, disappear."

"Well," I said, "I'll get the lorry first."

In the morning I took the first train to Damme. I had a room with a farmer. I had just arrived, taken my suitcase from the wardrobe, quickly thrown my things into it and was about to go to my car when a police officer arrived at the door. We knew him as we had been at the funfair in Damme the year previously.

He said, "Mr Winter, you must come with me." I asked why and acted dumb. "I must take you to Bremen."

"Why Bremen?"

"I must deliver you there."

"I haven't done anything!"

He hung around, "I still have to deliver you there. Bring your belongings with you. Actually, you are only allowed a knife and fork but bring your things with you."

I threw all my things into my case. Then I said to him, "Do me a favour! Can we do it like this: I walk to the station, you walk behind?"

"Can I trust you?"

"Of course. You can rest assured that I won't run away."

I walked to the station. He bought the ticket. I boarded the train. He travelled with me all the way to Bremen. He took me from the station to prison. We had to walk though the city centre. He even carried my case, as I was rather shaken up.

Fifty metres away from the prison he said, "You carry your case now. I'll be a laughing-stock if they see me carrying it."

In prison all my papers were taken from me. I was locked up in a prison cell. The door was locked shut. This was my end. After I had been sitting there for two hours a police officer came, returned my documents to me and said, "Come with me!" I was taken to an internment camp. I thought that at last there was the possibility of finding out where my brother and sister were. We arrived at Bremen's small harbour. We entered the so-called Coal Shed through the widely spaced planks of a gate. There was an office at the front where the police were sitting.

"What's your name?"

"Winter."

"Give me your papers." I handed him my papers. He leafed through everything: my trade licence, my sports card, everything. "Are you a Gypsy?"

"Yes, I wouldn't be here otherwise."

"Then join the others above." I heard children's voices. I went upstairs. They were all sitting there, men, women and children. The children were crying. It was frightful. Erich and Maria were there. After two days I went down to the police and asked if I could make a telephone call. I wanted to inform my parents. They allowed me to do that. My parents came to Bremen, they brought bedding and clothing, money too. The police said nothing and my parents were able to return home.

About five o'clock in the morning on the third day we had to assemble in the open. We were led to the station via a tunnel from the rear. A passenger train awaited us at the platform, guarded by SS men with rifles. We were told we were to be 'evacuated' to Poland. Each of us was to receive a piece of land which we would have to cultivate.

We thought, "Good, money we have, some clothing too. We will go along with this and then escape." We made such plans during the journey. Nothing came of them.

PART TWO

Auschwitz, Ravensbrück, Sachsenhausen

Aerial photograph of Auschwitz-Birkenau taken by an RAF reconnaissance pilot on 23 August 1944. Smoke can be seen billowing out of a mass burial pit.

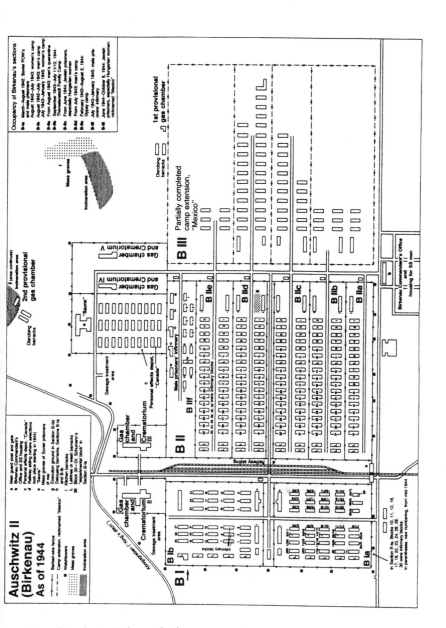

Plan of Auschwitz-Birkenau death camp.

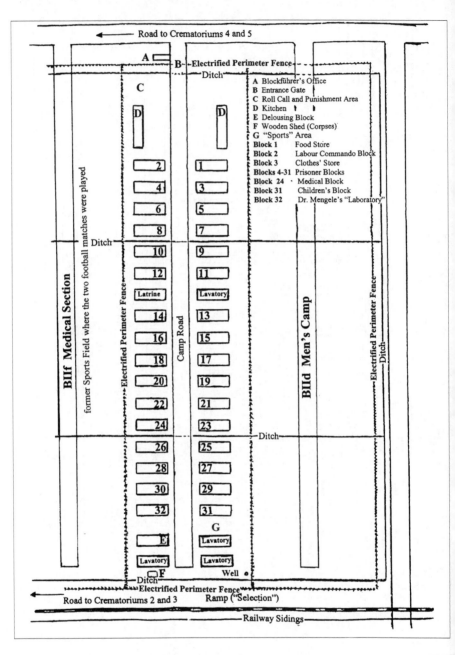

Plan of the Auschwitz-Birkenau "Gypsy Camp" BIIe.

Auschwitz-Birkenau

We travelled through the night and arrived in Auschwitz in the late afternoon of the following day. As we entered the station, the sidings and way were closed off with barbed wire. We shared our forebodings with one another. When the train came to a standstill we immediately heard, "Out, out, out, out!" A row of SS men with rifles stood there. "Out, out, out, out!" They dealt out kicks and blows with their rifle butts. "Faster, faster, faster!"

We were assembled in a five-row column and marched out of the station toward the camp. On the left side of the road stood war-damaged houses and I thought, "Heavens above, what's to become of us?" We arrived at Auschwitz concentration camp, at the main camp (Auschwitz I).[16] Here it was that I first read the sign: '*Arbeit macht frei*' ('work liberates'). We arrived as the work details marched in.

When we saw the columns of labourers I thought, "You aren't seeing right." They were carrying two corpses covered in blood. The corpses were slung from poles, tied by the hands and feet, like deer. Two men carried each corpse, streaming with blood. Our column became as quiet as a mouse despite there being children among us. You could have heard a pin drop. Having seen this we were so demoralized that we were unable to utter a word. We thought, "Is this going to happen to us? Oh God, oh God, oh God!"

I can no longer remember whether we had a one- or two-hour wait. Anyway, suddenly we heard, "All fall in." We then marched from the main camp to Auschwitz-Birkenau. It was late afternoon when we arrived in Birkenau. It was March.[17] We saw the camp, all the blocks[18] standing there. At this time, there was no perimeter fence. There was a squat bunker with guards to the right of the road. We were led through in two rows, where we got our prisoner number. Two people, one to each row, branded us with a number. We siblings stuck together. I received the number Z3105,[19] my brother Z3106, and my sister, among the women, the number Z3470.[20] We also had two cousins with us. We said to ourselves, "We must remain together if we can." After receiving a prisoner number we were allocated a block. Then we were two or three weeks in the blocks without a perimeter fence. It was open country. The SS had surrounded the area with machine-guns. Then perimeter fences and roads were built.

We were allocated to block 18. Each block had a 'Block Senior'.[21] These were mostly 'criminal' prisoners, sometimes 'political' prisoners.[22] The political prisoners were not particularly sweet-tempered either. They would shout, "Get a move on! Get a move on! Get a move on!" We stood there unable to comprehend what was happening. It was beyond description. We were completely mesmerised.

Three-tiered wooden bunks served as sleeping platforms; we were allotted a middle bunk. Ten men were crowded together on each bunk. We stood there speechless and helpless but we wanted to know what went on there.

A prisoner entered, a political prisoner, half-German half-Polish. He asked, "Where do you come from?"

"From Oldenburg. My brother, my sister, and my cousins."

To the rear of the camp area stood what I later I found out was the crematorium. We asked him, "What's that there?"

"Oh," he said, "that's an oven." He made such jokes.

He brought out a small bottle of vodka. "Come here and have a drink." He took a small glass from his pocket. He filled it and I knocked it back. I gasped for breath for it was 90 per cent vodka! That was his idea of a joke. We stuck with this man. He worked in the kitchen. We liked him and he liked us – especially my sister – and he provided us with food. His name was Leo Stachowiak. He told us that it had been his uncle, an engineer, who had constructed the Birkenau camp. Anyway, this uncle visited the camp every week or two. What Leo told us was confirmed later.

One day he said, "My uncle is coming today."

"How come your uncle's coming? Are you allowed visitors?"

"Yes," he said, "he's the engineer who built the entire camp. And I always give him things."

"What do you give him?"

"Diamonds, rings, gold."

This booty lay about at the Birkenau ramp, which was completed in 1943.[23] Until then the trains arrived at Auschwitz. We had alighted in the Auschwitz main camp. When the Birkenau track was completed, the Jews arrived here and had to throw all their belongings on the ground: bread, provisions, jewellery. This was collected in baskets. The provisions were used in the kitchen. Leo collected these provisions from the ramp. Then he said to us, "Here, soap". He had pressed the diamonds into the soap and then smeared over the surface. "I'll give this to my uncle, he will deliver half to my family."

Leo came from Katowice. His parents owned a bakery and a grocery. He was a political prisoner. He had been a fighter pilot. He was very good to us. Leo was released in 1944. We never heard from him again. He was probably conscripted again. Later we heard that his wife and children were alive.

For three months we had no water or toilets. We washed when it rained, making do in the puddles, this being our only chance of getting a little water on our faces. The women left the blocks at night to wash as best they could. Adults and children had to relieve themselves outside, to the rear of the blocks.

If I'm not mistaken, at the beginning, there was a corner

in Block 2 where, when you had money, you could buy drinks, non-alcoholic drinks. When there was no more money in the camp this drink counter disappeared.[24]

At the beginning the prisoner functionaries[25] were mostly criminal prisoners although several were political prisoners.[26] When we had been in our block about two weeks, these functionaries were removed and replaced with Sinti. As my brother and I had been in the Wehrmacht (the SS had our records), we were detailed, my brother as Block Senior and me as Roll Call Clerk.[27] We then ran the block. There were still no toilets and my brother Erich, as Block Senior, usually received a beating when the SS came and found the block dirty. We had no idea what to do with the excrement. We set up a toilet in the room at the rear of the block using long-handled, rectangular food bins from the kitchen. There were thirty-two blocks. Had every block taken only one bin there would not have been any bins remaining in the kitchen. The SS made a search. Firstly, we were beaten and then we had to clean the bins. What with? We wiped them out with grass or rags. Then the same bins came round again with our food in them. This happened during the first four to six weeks.

Concentration Camp Life

Delousing was repeatedly carried out in the camp. There were new arrivals daily who were deloused. We were 'booming', so to speak, with 700 to 800 people to a block – that is, 500 people too many. An entire family, ten, twelve, sometimes fourteen people slept in one bunk. They died like flies, particularly the children.[28] At the beginning, each child received a half litre of milk.[29] The Block Orderlies[30] distributed this. The Block Orderlies were boys who collected the food and saw that everything was shipshape in the block before the SS arrived. They also lined everybody up outside.

But despite the milk, these young children died. We had to register the deaths, so that the number of prisoners tallied, and lay them out in front of the block one beside the other: ten to fifteen children each night. The children gradually died until none were left, then the adults began to die. Eight, ten, twelve deaths each night. We had to collect them from the bunks and lay them out in front of the blocks. As Roll Call Clerk, I had to sign the death certificate: name, date of birth, and then my signature.

Sometimes we had to remove the bodies ourselves using a litter. At the rear, to the right of our camp, there was a crudely built wooden shed. Here we brought the corpses. Every evening, at five o'clock, after the workday was over and the labour details had marched back into the camp, a lorry arrived. At the beginning this was a lorry with trailer. When the camp was full, two lorries with trailers took the bodies away daily.

Once I had to load bodies, my cousin too. We were nabbed while walking down the camp road on the way to our block. "Come with us!" We had to help with the loading. The corpses were not lying on the loading surface but were piled high. You had to sling the corpse – "One, two, three!" – onto the top of the pile. Occasionally, the lorry was so laden that a corpse fell off on the other side. Now there were two lorries with what must have been thirty people loading the corpses.

I said to my cousin, "You know what, I'm going to beat it." It was dangerous to do anything that was not permitted, but I said, "I can't do this. I'm off. Are you with me?"

"Yes." We made ourselves scarce. Thank God, they didn't find out. Never again did I allow myself to be chosen for this work. Whenever the possibility arose I made myself scarce.

We prisoners were deloused every month. Then the women were forced to walk the length of the camp road entirely naked. They had to walk from their blocks, through the camp, to block 3 or 4, near the camp entrance. As punishment they had to walk the entire length of the road naked. Once we were assembled in front of the block when the women were to be deloused. Plagge, Roll Call Leader[31] for the Gypsy Camp and a murderer, Palitzsch, König and the Protective Custody Commander,[32] Dr Schwarzhuber, arrived.[33]

They yelled, "What's up? Why aren't you ready? Go back in and chase the women out!" We had to enter the block.

"Hurry up!" we said, "They're waiting outside, they'll soon come in with their rubber truncheons."

The women stood there naked, old women too, with whom I had been acquainted prior to Auschwitz. It was shameful, humiliating, you cannot imagine.

I was standing in front of the block when another delousing took place. The lads who made music had their musical instruments with them. These instruments were sacrosanct. The music was a help, a diversion, for those who still retained some of their senses. There wasn't anything else for them to look forward to in life. So, I was standing on the camp road, waiting for the people to leave the block before they lined up to march to the delousing.

The Block Commander's room[34] was situated near the camp entrance with a view of the road and all the blocks. Two lads with guitars stood in front of the block. These lads were posted to keep us informed of events and were known as 'camp telephones'. Our 'telephone' had just returned from relieving himself and had not noticed anything but Roll Call Leader Plagge had seen the two lads with guitars standing in front of the block. He came over. I saw him coming and I told the lads, "Get rid of those guitars or I'll get a bloody good hiding." They stepped back into the block and hid the guitars.

Plagge arrived. "And where are the two guitars?"

"What guitars?" I said.

"Two youths with guitars were standing here." He wasn't able to identify the two lads as he had been too far away. "Two youths were standing here holding guitars." He even showed me where. Of course it was true.

"I didn't see anything." I received my first slap in the face.

"Where are the guitars?"

I answered, "I haven't seen any."

"Bring me a stick!" I had to bring a spade handle. "Now do you know where the guitars are?"

"No."

"Bend over!" You had to count out when you got something on the backside. I counted to four, that much I remember and then I lost my senses. You no longer register anything anymore. You stand there numb and simply wait for ...

Then I felt a blow across the back of my neck and heard a voice: "Clear off."

I hadn't counted the blows, I could no longer count them;

there had been a great many. Blockführer König entered the block and found the guitars under a bunk.

There were no barriers of nationality among us prisoners. We got along with each other whether Polish, Ukrainian, French, Belgian or Dutch. There were no distinctions made, at any rate I never experienced any and I personally never made any. To be sure there were Poles who stole from fellow prisoners in the same block. At the beginning each person received a crust of bread and everyone rationed it for the day. You did not eat it all at once, you said, "Stop! This piece is for early tomorrow morning!" Some Poles stole this ration from their fellow prisoners. We had a few such people in our block. We couldn't stop these people. It achieved nothing when you gave one of them a beating, although I must say I reluctantly did this, very reluctantly. I did this principally because of the children. I felt so sorry for them because sometimes everything was stolen from them.

Our block was a mixture of nationalities.[35] We had Russian, or rather, White Russian Gypsies, Polish Gypsies, German Gypsies naturally, Hungarian Gypsies, Austrian Gypsies, Dutch, Belgian. No Italian, no Yugoslavian. I also met French Gypsies, musicians, a father with two sons. But they were in another block.

Between May and August 1944, the blocks on the left side of the Gypsy Camp were vacated. All the Sinti and Roma in these blocks had to move into the blocks on the right side of the road. Jews were quartered here as the SS had no alternative. To be blunt, they weren't being cremated quickly enough, the SS couldn't gas them quickly enough. These Jews were in our camp for a time but were also gassed later.[36]

From the beginning, in the spring of 1943, the transports arrived day and night. And we were shut in our blocks. The SS placed cudgels against the doors of the blocks, which were simple barn doors. But the SS couldn't carry on doing this as the work details had to leave in the mornings. So they no longer shut us in and we were able to follow everything that happened. The trains ... they arrived day and night.

There was curfew[37] during the work period when we were confined to the blocks and that meant from the time the work details marched out until 5pm when they returned. During this time you were not allowed to roam about unless you had something important to do such as bringing food to the blocks. However, I always moved about a little, to the rear of the blocks, and observed everything, including the ramp[38] and station.

We made one mistake. We didn't make a note of the names of the SS men but we didn't have pencils or paper. I was only able to write one letter, to my mother.[39] I wrote it on a scribbling pad. I no longer remember where I acquired this.

I never went any great distance from the Gypsy Camp. It was only in 1986, when we visited the Auschwitz–Birkenau memorial and museum, that I saw, for the first time, the size of the camp. To my knowledge it was in 1943 that work details moved out to build roads to Buna, to the huge chemical plant that had been constructed nearby.[40] Sinti and Roma were employed everywhere, everywhere. I was never a member of a work detail except for once in Crematorium 3 for one day. I then wangled my way out of this.

Football Matches

One day a new Roll Call Leader arrived. If I'm not mistaken his name was Hartmann, a man very keen on sport, an SS man naturally.[41] He asked around, the Block Senior, the Roll Call Clerks and the Block Orderlies, to identify those interested in sport: "Who plays football?"

Naturally, I was interested, along with other lads from East Prussia who had played in major clubs, and also my cousins.

He chose me as trainer and said, "You get together eleven or twelve footballers."

I must say that, in my opinion, this Roll Call Leader had a humane side to him. He supplied us with some provisions that he had probably 'organised'[42] by taking them from others. But we didn't give this a thought at the time, it being a matter of survival.

I selected footballers and trained them. At that time we had a sports field where later the male prisoners' infirmary, section BIIf, was built.[43] We organised ourselves, trained and made all the necessary preparations. The lads could play football, I saw this straight away but, unfortunately, we were short of a right winger. I couldn't find one, there was no one suitable. One day when we were training, two Jews were watching. There were some Jewish workers in our camp, in a separate block. One of them said, "I can play football." A short man, perhaps 5'5", 5'6" tall, he was slightly bow-legged. Well, we trained together and he was terrific.

The first match was arranged: Auschwitz Main Camp v.

Gypsies. There were six Polish national players in the Main Camp team. Kick off. Only a reduced SS presence remained in the camp, all the other SS men were at the sports field. SS lined the field on all sides as no prisoners were allowed to watch. Our camp lay directly adjacent to this sports field so we were able to watch. The electric current was switched off on the perimeter fence on the sports-field side. Everyone ran to the fence – the entire Gypsy Camp stood at the fence as spectators, with kith and kin, as the saying goes, or on the roofs of the blocks. The match began. We attacked from the start and scored the first goal after ten minutes. I thought, "Now all hell will break loose!" Normally the SS men from the Main Camp were rivals of those from Birkenau but at this moment they were sportsmen. As we scored our SS, the Birkenau SS, began to fire off their revolvers, like fireworks going off. So now, on, on! In the second half, we scored again. All hell *did* break loose! I thought, "Lad, if only you survive this!" The two SS factions began to abuse one another and were close to hitting each other. Shortly before the end we conceded a goal. We won 2–1. That eased things.

Hartmann, our SS man, who had made the whole thing possible, was naturally happy and a good sport. From then on he saw that we were better fed. I must say that we, these lads and I, always managed to barter or organise something, especially as we knew Leo in the kitchen. Everybody did this. It was because of this that these lads still had some flesh on their bones. They were all young lads and I was twenty-three. The packets we got from Hartmann fed us up a little. We played a return match and this time lost 2-1. But, oh, it was a terrific match.

Those were the football matches. Then the male prisoners' infirmary was built and the area was lost to us. That put an end to that but there was another reason. This Hartmann had two sons at the front and the man was well into his fifties at the time. He lost both sons. After that he was of no use to anyone anymore. Somehow, he was completely ... well, to lose two sons at one go is no trifle. Anyway, the football team was disbanded. But, when possible, we played among ourselves, between the blocks. We dared not be seen. But we knew, more or less, when Plagge or the other SS men cleared off, when they visited the town.

Guards and Prisoners

I lie awake nights and pictures from Auschwitz loom up. In the past few years it has got increasingly worse. At first I suppressed these things, now it's no longer possible. What you saw ...

One day Ilse Koch[44] entered the camp along the road with Palitzsch. She was dressed like a man and carrying a revolver. A close acquaintance of mine, from Osnabrück, was walking towards them carrying a briefcase. I always told myself, whenever SS personnel are on the road, never walk towards them. Whenever I saw one of them I immediately turned off into our block, behind a block or into another block. I *never* walked towards them because you could never gauge how they would react. My acquaintance approached with a briefcase under his arm and, I must say, that was stupid, for who had a briefcase in the camp? And it wasn't hard to guess that there was something in it. But he had done other similarly stupid things.

Koch called him, summoned him with her finger, because he had also forgotten to remove his cap. When you passed an SS man you had to remove your cap and step to the side as in the Wehrmacht. She called him to her and gave him a slap in the face, a real smack. He was knocked to the ground. He was fortunate that she did not mention the briefcase. She only said, "Can't you remove your cap?" and laughed derisively. She was a right bitch.

The guard on the perimeter fence by the newly dug drainage ditch alternated between the Block Senior, Block Orderlies, or Roll Call Clerk. Always two men right, two men left. Once I was standing by the fence on guard duty with someone when a young Jewish man with a briefcase walked by. The briefcase was full of cigarettes. He wanted to barter them in the male prisoners' infirmary.

I said to him, "Listen, go further down. If someone sees you, Plagge for example, I will get it in the neck and you know what that means."

"Yeh," he answered, "get lost!"

I said, "Not with me you don't!"

"Yeh," he repeated, "get lost!" This man was clerk to Pery Broad in the Political Department.[45] He was Broad's lackey; he sat in the orderly room of the Block Commander's room[46] at the front of the camp.

I said, "Don't be so cheeky, you get lost."

"What's your problem?" He tried to land a punch on me but I parried it. I landed him one which knocked him to the ground and I took the briefcase full of cigarettes. He cleared off but I knew this wasn't the end of the matter.

Ten minutes later I heard, "3105 report to the orderly room." I reported. He stood there. Broad sat behind his desk and asked, "What happened?" I told him what had happened. The lackey with the briefcase began to be insolent.

I said, "Don't talk to me like that, or I'll smack you in the gob again."

Broad stood up and yelled, "Quiet! I won't allow this here!" And to me, "Get out!"

Shortly thereafter Broad's clerk returned. He was on the other side of the perimeter fence in the quarantine section of the male prisoners' infirmary,[47] where he was to be sterilised. I now had to report to Bogdan. Bogdan was also a clerk in the Political Department but he was a political prisoner. He allowed me to enter and asked, "Where's the briefcase?"

I answered, "I have it in the block."

"I want it immediately."

I brought the briefcase to him and he then locked us in, he locked the door. He had a windowless room in his block partitioned off with boards. This Jewish prisoner, Bogdan and I were in here. They wanted to beat me up inside this dark room but I had my wits about me and sprang away from the door as they locked it from within. They then kicked and beat me but I didn't cop much. A woman from my block went to my room orderly, to my cousin, and told them, "They're beating up Walter in the block there." He came running and smashed open the door. As the door broke in I landed Bogdan such a blow that his lip was split open. Then the Camp Senior Hermann[48] arrived, a first-rate man. He was a great guy, a political prisoner. He worked tremendously hard on our behalf. He did not allow fights. He defended the Sinti. He snapped at Bogdan, "Your behaviour is totally unacceptable." Well, that was that.

My punishment was a day in the *Sitzbunker* (crouching cell). I was locked in from morning till evening. Broad ordered this. I was summoned to him regarding the cigarettes.

When his lackey began to lie again, I said, "Say that again and I'll give you one in the gob!" My reaction was impulsive.

Broad only said, "There will be no fighting here! Out!"

Consequently, I was shut up in this Sitzbunker. It wasn't possible to stand, you had to crouch the entire day. You had to crawl in and out through a hatch.

It was said that Broad was a very important person but he was only a member of the SS, no big shot. When selections[49] on the ramp or gassings or important meetings took place he never stood among the other SS officers, always somewhat to the rear. Nevertheless, even Leo, who had been there long before us, said, "He is the most important person of all those here in the Gypsy Camp. He is Gestapo." His office was in the SS barracks outside the entrance to the Gypsy Camp in the direction of crematorium 3. When the SS entered the Gypsy

Camp we had to play music and the women had to dance. Then the SS took their pleasure. Broad was usually in the party but never took part. He always kept his distance. I also never saw him hit anyone. He was a comparatively young man. I was older than he was.

The *Volksdeutsch*[50] members of the camp SS were the worst, these *Heim ins Reich*[51] people. They were absolute bastards – except one. His name was Beinski.[52] He fired his revolver in the air but I never saw him beat anyone. König, on the other hand, beat people recklessly.

Once I gave this Beinski a good bashing. That was a very dangerous thing to do but I acted impulsively. I did it because my inner voice told me, "You must do this." I was on night watch, fire watch. A drainage channel had been dug beneath the perimeter fence. This hole beneath the fence was guarded by Beinski – SS-Rottenführer Beinski. This evening we were a three-man watch in the Gypsy Camp. He had to stand on the other side of the fence and guard this hole.

He asked us, "Have you got a smoke?"

"Yes, we have."

"Then sling it over."

I said, "No, if you want a smoke then come over here." The hole was big enough to get through if you stooped.

"Well," he said, "I can't do that, I daren't do that. Sling it over."

"No."

"Alright, I'll come over." He took his rifle and threw it over to us. We couldn't use the weapon – that would have been suicide – so we put it to one side.

He came over to us, "Who's got the cigarette?"

I said, "Me," and hit him. The other two, to the left and right of me, gave this SS man a good beating too. Luckily it was a dark night, and we were standing in the shadow of the searchlight tower. We really gave it to him. Then we threw his rifle back over the fence and gave him a kick in the arse so that he returned through the hole. He landed in the mud.

We were terrified the next day. Had he or hadn't he

recognised one of us? The following day he went about the camp, searching everywhere, wearing sunglasses. Despite the glasses you could see the bruises on his face. It was a hell of a risk we took for he could have simply shot us but the hate was uncontrollable. We were convinced we wouldn't leave there alive. We had seen so many dead. But we got away with it. Had Beinski known or noticed anything, something would have happened to us the next day. We were relieved when the day was over. We had got through the day without incident. That was something. When we were able to carry out an act of sabotage, or some form of resistance, we did.

When the SS wanted their pleasure they took women from the blocks. The man from whom I had taken the cigarettes came looking to take a woman. My brother was Block Senior, and told him, "Not from my block!" whereupon he tried to punch Erich. Erich hit him over the head with a spade handle and broke his collarbone.

I even saw an SS man with tears in his eyes. This was to do with one of our relatives, a musician from Berlin. He had studied at the conservatory and played several instruments. We buried him. What do I mean "bury"? We accompanied him with a Sinti band to the shed at the rear where the corpses were thrown. The boys played wonderful melancholic music. They were terrific musicians. The SS men stood near and this SS man, who was not from our camp, a young man of my age, turned away. I saw the tears running down his cheeks. He turned away and went off on his own. I was standing on the side and observed this. He stopped watching and walked straight out of the camp. Not all the SS were indifferent. They were in a dilemma but I condemn what they said after the war. They all said, "I was simply following orders." Or, "If I had not done as ordered I would have been imprisoned in a concentration camp myself." That is a pathetic excuse. They would have been transferred but not imprisoned in a concentration camp.

We had an SS man who posted our mail for us. He also received letters and parcels for us in his name. That was very dangerous. But he was from Oldenburg. We also had lived in Oldenburg. He was roughly the same age as my brother and before the war often went to dances with us in Oldenburg. He knew my brother better than me for I was still a boy at the time. He was courting the daughter of a showman and later married her. He was the kitchen chef. Leo was in charge of the kitchen, but he was the chef. Leo had told him, "There are people here from Oldenburg named Winter."

He pricked up his ears, "Winter? From Oldenburg? I know them!" That very same evening after curfew he came to us in the camp asking, "Where can I find the Winter family?" He found us and greeted my brother, "Hell, Erich, that we should meet here!"

Our parents had no idea where we were. After nine months in Birkenau this man took a letter from us to our parents when he went home on leave. He brought letters on his return and later received parcels with provisions and letters addressed to him, on our behalf, which he brought to us in the evenings after curfew when he was on duty. It was very risky but I want it to be known that this man did this for us as we knew him personally. He always brought us some food when he came. He was a minor SS man, I think he was a Rottenführer, like a lance corporal in the Wehrmacht.

Camp Punishment

Leo Stachowiak was smitten with my sister. One day he came and said to her, "Come to the kitchen tomorrow morning and I will give you something to eat." He always brought us something when he could. My sister went to the kitchen the next day. You had to sneak there. You could not say, "I'm just going to the kitchen, see you later!" That was impossible. You had to be inconspicuous. He gave her a bone. I no longer remember whether it was from cow or calf. Anyway, it was a thick bone and you could do a lot with it. You could secretly make soup with it.

My sister had concealed the bone behind a piece of rag. We had fastened this rag to a bunk as a curtain. We had placed our few belongings behind this curtain. Unthinkingly, she had laid the bone here. I didn't know about it. Neither did my brother Erich. Then Plagge arrived. As always he came and inspected the blocks after the work details had marched out. With König, Beinski or someone else. Then, when something wasn't to his liking, or when he was in a bad mood, there were slaps in the face or kicks up the arse, so to say, or clubbings. That was a daily occurrence. By chance he lifted this curtain, took the bone, and asked, "Where did this come from?"

My sister answered, "I was given it as a present."

"Who gave it to you?"

"I don't know, it was on the camp road." There were more than 20,000 people in the Gypsy Camp. "Someone gave it to me on the camp road."

"You're lying."

More questions and answers. Plagge then told her she would receive a flogging on the rack.

My brother said, "Take me; I'll take the flogging in her place."

Plagge carried a thin cane, like schoolteachers in the past. He asked my brother, "Who gave you the bone?" When an SS man spoke to you, you had to stand at attention, cap off, hands held by the seams of the trousers. Erich had to do this.

Plagge took the cane and when Erich said, "I don't know!" he stabbed him with the cane. He tried to stab out his eyes. Each time Erich drew his head away.

"Keep your head still! And I want to know where the bone came from!" Again and again and again. In the end, Erich looked like someone with chicken pox.

Maria and I beseeched him, "Herr Plagge, it was a soldier!" And so forth.

In between he also asked me where the bone came from. I answered, "I don't know."

Maria stuck to her story. She had to report to the Block-führer's office. The entire kitchen personnel had to report, Leo Stachowiak among them. Maria had to inspect the row. Leo was among them.

Plagge said, "He must be here!" Plagge had received a tip-off from someone.

She passed along the line and at the end said, "He's not here."

Plagge answered, "You're lying, look again."

She had to inspect the line again. "No, he's not here!"

Then my brother had to report. He received a flogging. The rack stood on the roll-call area at the front of the camp and he was strapped to it. Afterwards he couldn't sit for eight days, he had to lie on his stomach. I massaged him with the butter we received. I used a little of this as a salve. He was blue-green. It was indescribable.

Plagge and König had told the Protective Custody Commander Palitzsch that my brother had taken the flogging for our sister. Such a thing was unheard of in the camp! That a brother took the flogging for a sister had never happened before. Palitzsch arrived at our block and entered. We reported. We three stood there. He asked us our names, who we were and what we had done previously. Pleasantries.

Then my sister said, "Ah, so you're Herr Palitzsch. You're the man we're all terrified of. You shoot people."

I thought, I'm not hearing right! My brother and I spoke to her in our language,[53] "You shouldn't have said that. Keep quiet!" But she didn't stop.

He looked at her and laughed, "Well," he said, "that's what you think?"

"Yes!"

"That's what you think?" I tugged her from behind but it was no use. She reacted impulsively.

He listened to her again and laughed, "Well, if you believe that!" He had a few more words with us and departed. He was gone.

I said, "Watch, you'll be called to the flogging rack now. Did you imagine he wouldn't retaliate?"

But he did not return.

My sister's intention was to get him to stop shooting people but it was impossible to influence these people. Perhaps she also wanted to provoke him, entice him out of his shell. Perhaps she wanted to try her luck. My brother and I simply stood there. I was relieved when Palitzsch left. I expected the call, "Block 18, number so-and-so to the Blockführer's office!" I waited for this. But thankfully it didn't come.

I don't think that in 1943–44 the SS men believed that Nazi Germany was going to win the war. That's why they acted as they did. They thought, "We are dead one way or the other." After the war Schwarzhuber was condemned. Palitzsch was condemned.

Hartmann, our Roll Call Leader, became a completely different person after his two sons were killed and not only with regard to myself and the other footballers. Prior to this he had been a reasonable person who didn't tolerate anyone being beaten. After the death of his sons he suddenly finished with the football matches. Now the male prisoners' infirmary stood where the football field had been. Here lay the corpses which were removed by lorry each evening.

I haven't mentioned that there was a 'sports area' in the Gypsy Camp. This was not in the normal sense of 'sport' but sport in the sense of inflicting pain.[54] This area was situated behind the last block on the left side of the road, if I'm not mistaken, behind block 30 or 31. The SS had had pebbles dumped here, large pebbles. We had to do 'sport' here: head-stands, running on our knees, rolling over, crawling on our elbows. The SS men walked on us. The old men were left dead. When they didn't roll over quickly enough the SS ran over their bodies as though they were railway sleepers. Especially König, the murderer.

Collaborators

I now want to talk about collaborators.[55] There were such people among us Gypsies, there were such people among the Jews; they are to be found everywhere. Several collaborators joined us in Birkenau. Apparently their papers preceded them. We knew this a week or two before their arrival. Our Camp Senior Hermann informed us. Hermann got on well with Jósef Cyrankiewiecz,[56] he gave him useful information. After the war Jósef Cyrankiewiecz became prime minister of Poland. He told us, "Another collaborator is arriving." This collaborator came from Vienna, an Austrian who had been a member of the criminal police. He deserved to have been hanged. That would have been his just desert. Had he been a Pole or a Russian they would have hanged him. They showed no mercy. We didn't do that but he got a beating from everybody. He was given a rough time and not only from the Sinti and Roma but from the SS too. They usually didn't like collaborators either. His face was a pulp. His mouth had been full of gold teeth, afterwards he was toothless. That was justified as he had betrayed our people to the police. He was a despicable collaborator. Then several minor collaborators arrived but perhaps the police had forced these people to collaborate. You couldn't tell.

One came from Hannover. His daughter was already in the camp. I had known this man from my childhood on. He was an elderly man. We were informed, "He will arrive tomorrow. You know what to do." This spread from block to block. He arrived. I was on the camp road, having probably come out of another block, when Thomas Höllenreiner,[57] a Sinto from Munich, came towards me.

"Lad." He spoke the thick Bavarian dialect. "Go inside, the collaborator has arrived. I've boxed his ears for him." He had given him a good clouting.

I answered, "Enough said." I went to him. I had seriously intended to give him a good going over.

I entered the block and saw this man I knew from home. He was the brother of the uncle married to my mother's sister. He sat there with a swollen face and with tears in his eyes. His daughter sat next to him with her arms around him supporting him. When I saw him I had misgivings. I thought, "This is a collaborator? I don't believe it, it can't be true!" I pushed all this to one side as I knew that he came from Hannover and could give me information about my parents. This was before we had contact with them through the SS man from Oldenburg. I said to myself, "Now you can find out how they are!" I must be honest, I wouldn't have been able to hit the man. I had known him since I was a child.

"Hello," I said but naturally didn't offer him my hand. "You are from Hannover and my uncle is Uncle Hans." This was his brother. "Where are my parents? How are they?"

He in turn asked, "Well, lad, who are you then?" I hadn't introduced myself to him. He was repugnant to me but I had known him since I was a child. "Your parents are at home." He knew everything about them. "Your uncles too, and your aunts. They're all at home."

I breathed a sigh of relief. I experienced a pleasant, weightless feeling. I didn't question him further, but spoke only of trivial things and then left. I never wanted to see him again.

The Poles reacted differently. When they were informed that a collaborator had arrived he was immediately hanged. Well, to be perfectly honest, I couldn't have done such a thing. When you see someone who you have known since a

child and he is the brother of your uncle ... No. I never visited or spoke to this man again. He no longer existed for me.
He had collaborated with the police.

Children

For a while I had thirty parentless children in my block. These children were so emaciated I could no longer bear to see them. It was because of these children that I would not condone the theft of food in our block. Although not permitted I made a table from the wooden bunks at the back of the block that, for the time being, were empty with so many having died. I rammed the uprights into the ground and placed planks on top so that the children were able to sit alone to eat, under the eyes of a Room Orderly. Despite this the food was insufficient. The children were demoralised, they were completely alone. I took care of these children. They were my darlings.

One day the children were again robbed of their food. We considered the situation.

I said, "It is unacceptable that the children's food is stolen, I'm going to Mengele."[58] It was this man who determined what happened to the children.

I was told, "Man, you can't go to him. He'll shoot you." This was an expression of the fear people had.

I said, "I'm going to him."

I often saw him arriving by motorbike. The infirmary blocks[59] were on the right side of the camp road. Mengele was there from time to time during the day. I entered.

There was a Polish doctor who said to me, "Are you really going in to him?"

I answered, "Yes, I have thirty starving children. Let him

know I wish to see him."

He knocked on Mengele's door. I was told to go in. I entered, stood to attention in front of him – I had been a soldier – reported, named the block, and informed him about the children.

He said, "I'll come by this afternoon and have a look at the children."

He came. The children had to line up. Then, by chance, he noticed a girl standing in the front whose parents were still alive, but this little girl was as emaciated as the others. He told me to stand her up on the stove in the block.

He observed her and then asked, "How old is this girl?"

I'm sorry to say that we didn't know her age but we had index cards. We gave him our estimate according to her height.

He said, "All right." Then he wrote me out a note. "An extra container of food for these children."

We dished this out to the children, under supervision. From time to time I was also present. These little children wolfed it down until they couldn't eat any more. In spite of this extra food, many became ill and died and, after a few months, all the children in the camp had died. At least they had this supplementary food and we adults received what was left over. We shared this out.

I never allowed myself to be dissuaded from intervening. That's why I went to Mengele about the food. Perhaps it was foolishness, perhaps it was courage but I don't know of another Sinto who had the courage to speak to an SS man in this way.

My sister had twins. One of the two had one light and one dark eye.[60] My sister didn't have her children by her for long in the camp as Mengele took them. At this time the infirmary blocks on the right side of the road were established. We never saw the children again. Never again. They were lovely children, around seven or eight years old.

I must tell you about two little boys. I didn't know them

by name but one was seven or eight, the other was perhaps ten or eleven. This was shortly before Leo Stachowiak's release.

He said to me, "Walter, I must go to the ramp tomorrow, I need to collect bacon fat and sausage and other food." The Jews were 'selected' on the ramp as soon as they arrived: the sick, the old, women and children were selected for gassing and they went directly to the crematoria. Among them were people who threw away everything they possessed – bread or sausage or bacon fat, whatever they had – and Leo had to collect this and bring part of it to the kitchen. It was carried in baskets.

He said to me, "Come to block 32 early in the morning. And I will look for salami" – firm Hungarian salami sausage – "and bacon fat, and sling it over the fence to you." But there were sentries[61] in the watchtowers. In the meantime, the prisoners had dug a drainage ditch. This ditch was dug adjacent to the camp road, the entire length of the camp, because the ground was very muddy and wet.

Next morning I went and stood behind the block at the rear of the camp with some other prisoners. I saw how Leo picked something up and threw it into the basket. Whenever he thought he had found something we could use, he threw it behind him. He couldn't do anything else as the SS were 'selecting' Jews as they got off the train, while other SS men stood around keeping watch over everything. Leo was too far from the perimeter fence, between the first and second railway lines where the belongings lay. These two young lads were with me and they wanted to run to where Leo had thrown something behind him that had landed on the other side of the fence. I saw how, each time, the lads wanted to run to wherever the things Leo had thrown had landed. "Stay here!" I warned them a number of times.

Then Leo threw a sausage that landed in the so-called off-limits zone. This was the zone between the electrified perimeter fence and the inner fence, which was only a single strand of wire roughly seventy centimetres from the ground. Anyone entering this off-limits zone was shot dead by the guards in the watchtowers. The lads ran and I yelled, "Stop, stay here, stay here!" They leapt over the six-foot-wide drainage ditch, grabbed the sausage and leaped back. As they hit the side of the ditch the guard in the right watchtower shot at them. He hit the older boy in the hand and the younger in the heart. He lay there dead. The older boy, who had been wounded in the hand, also remained lying on the slope. I ran to him, lifted him up and took him to the infirmary block. Jewish doctors worked there.

I went in to the infirmary and said, "Here, they have just shot him." The doctor examined the shattered hand. The wound was from a kind of dumdum bullet that had shattered everything, the fingers and all the bones.

He said, "We can't repair it." The lad whimpered but did not cry out. The doctor said, "I must operate." And to me, "You must remain here, and assist me, I have no assistants." He lay the lad down and I held the shattered hand. Then he explained, "Here, we'll leave the thumb but the fingers must be removed." He removed the fingers, left the thumb, and bandaged up the hand. I then took the lad to his block. I think he was an orphan. His parents were dead. I asked after him a number of times, I also spoke to him. Suddenly he was gone, no longer there. I don't know what happened to him.

Shootings, Hangings

One afternoon, after work was over, Plagge and his lackeys arrived with a stretcher. Two prisoners had to carry this litter on which lay a Gypsy whom I knew as he came from Mannheim. He had gunshot wounds. Plagge went from block to block. He also came to us and said, "Everyone, come here and see this! The same will happen to others who attempt to escape." This continued from block to block. The man was riddled with bullet holes. I don't believe this occurred while he was escaping but after he had been caught. They riddled him with shots. It was terrible to witness. When you got up in the morning you didn't know if you would see the end of the day.

On another afternoon gallows were erected in the section where the Polish Jews[62] were held. We all had to go to this side of the camp and watch. Two men were hanged. The Commandant of Auschwitz Höß[63] was present, our commander Schwarzhuber, Broad from the Political Department and many other SS men. The two Poles had to stand on stools. Höß passed sentence and asked them if they wished to say anything. One said nothing, the other, a young lad, shouted, "Long live Poland!" Then they kicked away the stools. I was forced to observe such scenes several times.

One evening Beinski and König arrived during curfew. Curfew meant we had to nip inside the blocks, like lightning, when the bell went at 10pm. And the children ... you know how it is. If this didn't proceed exactly to the liking of the SS they shot into the air. Beinski had a woman in his sights, who he … these curs, these murderers, had no shame, they took women from the blocks, used them and were through with them. Beinski had designs on this woman but she had a partner, they were a couple. Beinski knew precisely where her bunk was. He shot through the block wall from outside and killed the woman.

It was Christmas Eve 1943. We were sitting together after curfew. Each was lost in his own thoughts, thinking of home, of his parents or brothers and sisters. Our 'camp telephone' also had to be inside the block by ten, you were not allowed to be outside. Suddenly the door opened and two men ran in. I must say I didn't actually see them myself. I really didn't. Then Plagge arrived. I reported as usual.

He asked, "Where are the two men who ran in here?"

"I didn't see anyone." I was at the front of the block where I had partitioned off a section with blankets so that I could keep the files for the block and do the paper work.

Anyway, I hadn't seen anyone. He threatened me, "Then I must count out ten people." People were sitting on the stove. You must picture this stove. There was a tall stove whose chimney didn't run directly upwards but horizontally, at seat height, the entire length of the block and out the back. There was a similar stove at the back of the block, whose chimney ran the length of the block in the opposite direction and out the front. These flues served as seating along the middle of the block. Plagge picked ten men from here, "You, you, you, you … come here!" He had them stand in front of the block. "So, I'm now going to shoot you all!"

A Jew, a tall man, was standing behind these ten. When he saw that they were to be shot he said, "It was me! I was the one."

"Come here!" Plagge took his revolver, turned him round and asked him, "Who was the other man?"

"I don't know him," answered the Jew. I believed him for his life depended on it. No one else came forward; perhaps he had run through the block and out the other end. The first man insisted, "I don't know him." He said it over and over again. Perhaps I would have done the same and not betrayed anyone. I was also someone who would have rather taken the blame before informing on anyone.

Then Plagge said, "Right, I'm going to shoot you." He turned to me and said, "and you come too." We walked to the fence. Plagge said to the Jew, "So, get under the fence." This was the single strand of wire before the electrified fence two metres beyond it. He had to pass beneath the wire so that it appeared he was attempting to escape. Plagge took his revolver and held it to the Jew's mouth, "If you don't tell me now who the other man was, I'll shoot you."

The Jew repeated, "I don't know who it was." I really believe that he didn't know who it was. In such a situation I would perhaps have said, "I saw him but I don't know him." He said again, "I don't know the man." Plagge pulled the trigger. He fell dead.

"So," said Plagge, "now it's your turn." At that moment my mind went blank. I had a blackout, a complete blackout. Had Plagge then said, "Get yourself beneath the wire!" I would have followed his order, sheep-like, would have stood there and he would have shot me.

"Were you a soldier?" he asked me suddenly.

"Yes." Plagge visited the blocks every morning and I always reported to him correctly, as in the Wehrmacht. Perhaps he remembered this.

"Where?" he continued.

"In the navy, in Wilhelmshaven."

"And what were you before that?"

"A showman."

"Hmm," was his only reaction. "Hmm." Then he talked normally to me. I was in line to be shot. As I stood before him, our eyes met for a few seconds. "Clear off!" he said abruptly. I ran into the block. I took deep breaths. So. I sat there. It was Christmas Eve.

Gassings

In the first weeks, during the spring of 1943, we had to remain shut up inside the blocks and when the wind was blowing from the direction of the crematoria the stench was unbearable. Six- or seven-metre high flames rose from the chimneys. The chimneys burst. Later they were reinforced with iron rings. When, after four weeks, we were let out of the blocks because the first labour details were to leave the Gypsy Camp, we saw the transports. It was continuous: arrival, unloading, departure, then on to the next transport – day and night.[64]

When you went to sleep in the evening you wondered, "Will I wake up here in the morning?" Two transports of Gypsies were gassed. Both times those blocks selected to be gassed were only a block away from ours. Once we heard, "Typhus threat".[65] Transports arrived and two blocks were gassed. We asked ourselves, "What shall we do? When they come – I'm not getting onto the lorry. I'll find some men who are still fairly fit." We chose thirty men and made a plan. We knew exactly how the SS proceeded. They flung open the door and stormed in shouting, "Out, out, out!" We agreed, "If they come to us we'll stand behind the door, we'll let them storm in, we'll die one way or the other, it doesn't matter how. We'll grab them." There would not be that many, five or six men: "We'll grab them. One of us will get his hands on a machine gun somehow or other, it doesn't matter how, and finish off as many as we can. We have nothing to lose, we are destined for the crematoria one way or the other."

We were ready and waiting behind the door. The SS were in the last block before ours. One of us kept a lookout from a ventilation slit over the top bunk, in the otherwise window-less blocks. I also took my turn as lookout. Plagge was there, König, Beinski, Broad and Palitzsch. When they were finished with this block, the people were loaded onto lorries and driven to the gas chambers. We could see the gas chambers, crematoria 2, 3, 4 and 5. The lorries drove out past our block, to our left, directly to the gas chamber.

Suddenly, someone arrived on a motorbike and, we did not know why, the operation was broken off. The lorries drove away with the people from the last transport. We waited. Silence. The entire block. At this time we were still 500 or 600 people and the whole block held its breath, quiet as a mouse. Strange: there were also still a few young children with us, but they made no sound, all deathly quiet. This was how it was with the first gassing.

The second time, months later, Russian Gypsies arrived. Again two blocks. Again curfew. The SS shut the doors and bolted them from outside. Then they drove all the people in the two blocks diagonally opposite ours onto the lorries. "Get up! Get up! Get up!" With rifle butts and kicks up the arse. "Move! Move! Move!" We watched from the windows above. We did as we had done the first time and assembled the men who were still fairly fit. Again the operation was over when these two blocks were cleared. Palitzsch arrived by motorbike and drove among them. The last had to jump up onto the lor-ries. The SS officers came together and whispered to one another but we could not hear what they said. Then they drove off in their vehicles. That was the second gassing. Two blocks, a thousand individuals.

My brother Erich was the first of us to get typhus. This was at the time when the Russian Roma arrived. It was said that they had brought typhus with them but, at the same time, we also received large, red woolly blankets. Several people contracted typhus. Erich was taken to the infirmary block. He couldn't eat and was delirious. There were single bunks in the infirmary block. The infirmary block was separately enclosed and it was only possible to enter it from the front. In the evenings we sneaked in, Maria or I, because it would have been more difficult for two people to do this. Leo helped us get milk and we poured this down his throat. The Jewish doctor in the infirmary block turned a blind eye.

One evening Erich lay there with his arm hanging down outside the bed. There was blood on the floor. He had attempted to cut his arteries. He had broken the bottle in which we had brought him milk and had hacked his wrist. In his delirium he had imagined he was being taken to the gas chamber and that they wanted to murder him. In his delirium he had preferred to kill himself. He told us this later. However, he hadn't cut the arteries, only the skin. There were no bandages so we wrapped his wrist with toilet paper. We nursed him through it.

We then took him out of the infirmary block. He couldn't walk, he couldn't do anything anymore. When you have typhus you are as helpless as a child. You even have to learn to walk again. Just when he was able to walk to a certain degree again, I myself contracted typhus and was taken to the infirmary block. Luckily, Maria didn't succumb to typhus. Erich and Maria nursed me and pulled me through. But I know how it is: you are delirious, you are bedridden with a high fever, a very high fever. Otherwise, nothing, you can do nothing, nothing.

Each morning we had to form up in ranks. The roll-call area lay between the blocks. Here the people were assigned to work details. The people marched to the roll-call area and assembled; the band played and the labour details departed the camp to a musical accompaniment. At the count, as roll-call clerk and Block Orderly, I stood at the front. The Block Orderlies had to see that everyone was standing in rows of five.

One morning there were ten men short for the detail at

crematorium 3. Plagge came and commandeered ten men, me amongst them. I spent a day at the crematorium. For the first time I saw the scale of it all, how the people ... what it was like there. Prior to this I had imagined that they made a fire into which they threw the bodies. I arrived at the crematorium and we were assigned tasks. Two men to fetch wood, the others had to drag the corpses from the gas chamber. Always two or three men. I was assigned to fetch wood. I fetched the wood from the side of the crematorium. The wood was laid beneath these furnaces. The people were dragged out of the so-called shower room. Sometimes it was impossible to separate the corpses. They had an iron pole, like a meat hook, with an S shaped hook and a ring. The corpses were so rigidly entangled with one another... I stood there and looked on. At that moment the SS man wasn't there, he was elsewhere talking with other SS men. I stood before the furnaces and saw everything. They dragged two men from the gas chamber, they couldn't part them. They had to break or hack off their arms. They then stacked them onto the pan. Normally, one or two corpses were stacked here but they stacked four to six corpses one on top of the other. I looked once and couldn't look anymore. I simply brought the wood, tipped it out, stacked it and drove away again. I did this for a day. The next day I said to myself, "You're not going back there again."

I knew that these labour details had to work for a period of three months there. I heard from the Jewish prisoners that all those who worked in the crematoria were themselves gassed and cremated at the end of three months. I decided, "I'm not going to be a part of this." Luckily for me, the next morning the SS took others from elsewhere. This was the only time I worked at the crematorium and that sufficed. You could see how people had, in their clamour to rise above the gas, scratched into the walls of the gas chamber with their fingernails. They were entangled, three or four together, with children, rigidly entangled. This crematorium was perhaps

200 metres away from the Gypsy Camp. We could clearly see when the SS man arrived wearing a mask. A slope led up to the top of the gas chamber where the SS man then opened a hatch and tipped in the poison, Zyklon B.[66]

There is the story of a woman, a French actress. We knew this because Beinski, this 'Volksdeutsche' SS man told us. He had some kind of contact with us Gypsies because he was infatuated with our women. He told us that all had to completely undress before entering the 'shower room'. There was an adjacent room, the SS took the women here and raped them, this actress too. This woman was clever. She entered and they ripped off her brassiere and she had to lower her trousers. An SS man stood beside her. She pulled out his revolver and shot two of them. Well, she was dead one way or the other. This made me feel good.[67]

Then there were the unfortunate people on their way to the crematorium. One night I lay awake when I heard the barking of dogs and shooting. Transports arrived, the deportees had to jump down onto the track as there was no platform. The way to crematorium 3 led past the Gypsy Camp. There were bunkers with SS guards en route. This particular night the people found out that they were destined for the crematorium. They resisted and the SS mowed down the entire column. Every single person. Everyone on the road was shot dead.

Between May and August 1944 countless Jews were gassed and cremated. Presumably the SS and German industry required fewer workers. The SS 'selected' people for work, including young lads of fourteen or fifteen. They passed themselves off with, "I'm sixteen", "I'm seventeen".

Long narrow trenches were dug to the rear of the crematoria because the chimneys had burst from burning ash and heat, from being in operation day and night. The SS were unable to gas the mass of people. The corpses were thrown into these trenches with wood and tar, or whatever, on top and set alight. Shot and dumped, or dragged from the gas chambers and thrown into these holes in the ground. If you should visit Auschwitz and stand in front of the former Gypsy Camp, look right. Crematorium 3 was situated behind the male prisoners' infirmary, section BIIf. Today birch trees grow behind this crematorium. Then there was neither tree nor shrub, only open ground. These mass graves are there.

The gassing of the Jews operated non-stop, day and night, so that on many days we were no longer able to breathe. And, this stench of burning flesh! Mountains of ash, four or five metre high mounds, adjacent to the crematoria.

Shoes

In May 1944 we had to vacate the blocks on the left side of the Gypsy Camp and move into the blocks on the right. At this time there were only about 250 people left alive in these blocks. 'Selected' healthy Jewish men from the transports then occupied these blocks. At the beginning these people wore civilian clothes but were also issued with a zebra-striped uniform. The Hungarian Jews had wonderful boots, beautiful laced boots. We were running around in wooden clogs. We immediately saw that these Jews were not 'selected' for forced labour. They had to fall in block-wise, were led to the camp entrance and to the crematorium. Each morning one or two blocks departed. We witnessed this. They asked us about the situation, where they were destined and what would be expected of them. I was unable to tell these people the truth.

What should I have said? I said, "You must work here."

"Yes, but … those that left yesterday have not returned."

"They will probably have been given a block elsewhere." Or such like. I simply couldn't tell them the truth.

I want to come back to the fact that the Hungarian Jews had beautiful boots. I now saw Sinti and Roma walking about in such boots. In the block directly opposite mine there were many people wearing these beautiful boots. I went over, with bread I could spare, although I was also hungry. I wanted a pair of those boots. I went over.

"Can we barter?"

"No, we can't. I need my boots."

I didn't say, "You won't need them any more." I just couldn't say this. I went back and forth. They were hungry too. Finally, I said, "Here, take this piece of bread. I'll bring you this evening's ration too if you give me your boots. I'll also give you the shoes I'm wearing. You don't need to go barefoot." He agreed and I took the boots. Next day they were gassed. The block was led out and they ended up in the crematorium, including the man with whom I had spoken and his son. The boy was fifteen, he had probably passed himself off as being older. All ended up in the crematorium, every last one, until the blocks on the left side of the camp were empty.

This is essentially what we experienced in Auschwitz-Birkenau. There are things that happened that for a moment you don't remember but when you start to recount the event the whole experience comes to mind. You were so hardened that you said, "When they decide to gas us, I'm not getting onto the lorry." I planned this with my brother Erich, my sister Maria, and my cousins. We were all agreed. "We'll try to grab a revolver or machine gun from one of them. We'll mow down the SS and then kill ourselves." Or, "I'll run onto the fence, grasp the fence." The perimeter fence was charged with 500 volts. "They're not going to have the pleasure of shooting or gassing me."

Then the Day Arrived

I had contact with Jósef Cyrankiewiecz.[68] I got on well with him and we exchanged information. Transports left for Buchenwald, for Flossenbürg.[69] I wanted to be among them, I wanted to get out of Auschwitz but he told me, "Walter, stay here as long as possible. I'll let you know when. When I say you should get out, then it'll be time."

When there were gassings, as Roll-Call Clerk I had to take all the index cards in a small box I had made to the orderly room[70] at the front of the camp.

I asked, "What's going on? Are we going to be gassed?"

The answer was, "No, probably one block will be gassed." These were the Russian Gypsies.[71]

Then the day arrived. The day finally arrived. It was the beginning of August 1944.[72] We were told that all former Wehrmacht soldiers could take their family members with them on the transport out. When we were deported to Auschwitz there were about 500 former Wehrmacht soldiers. Now that we were to leave there were perhaps 150 of us still alive. Things started to happen. We all had to fall in. We were allowed to take only our immediate family with us, parents, brothers, sisters, aunts, uncles, cousins. Well, nearly all parents had died. Not mine, thank God, they were at home. Schwarzhuber stood at the front at a kind of lectern and read out the prisoner numbers of former Wehrmacht soldiers and then you had to say, "He and she are my cousins ... " We were out. Lorries stood outside the camp onto which we were to be loaded. They drove in the direction of Auschwitz Main Camp, not in the direction of the crematorium. My number was called out twice, my wife was somewhere in the camp and I had had to look for her not knowing where she was at that moment. My sister, my two cousins and some others already stood behind me. I couldn't take the entire block. I would have done so had it been possible. I took everyone that I could.

I finally found my wife in our block. Everything was in a state of confusion. She was the cousin of my brother Erich's wife. It happened so, young men fit for work were repeatedly deported to other camps, to Buchenwald, to Dachau, everywhere where workers were needed. And it was said that only married men could stay with their families. My brother's wife came up with the idea and said, "Walter, my cousin is in such and such a block. You don't need to get married, simply get yourselves on the list of married couples." Many people did this. I had just left the typhus block and was still unable to walk properly when this girl came over to us in our block. Everything then took place very quickly. She was in agreement. As Roll-Call Clerk I simply wrote that she was my wife and that we were married according to Sinti custom. This was accepted. It is Sinti custom that both fathers give their consent to the marriage. The prospective husband first goes to the woman's father and asks for his daughter's hand in marriage. Having received the consent of both fathers the couple must live a year with the wife's parents and then a year with the husband's parents. A registry office or church wedding is then unnecessary. This wasn't possible in our case. It was more a marriage of convenience. This made it possible for me to stay together with my brother, sister and cousins. You did not know what awaited you in another camp and it was better to be together with other family members. My wife Anna then moved into our block. She was able to swap blocks with another prisoner. She was a lovely girl, completely loyal to me. We were able to stay together until we reached Ravensbrück.

Then a close acquaintance from home came to me. She was a member of the Blum family. She had a husband and a six-month-old baby. I felt someone tug the back of my jacket. "Walter, take us with you." She spoke in our language. I said, "Damn it all!" Then my number was called out a third time. I had not yet reported as not all those whom I wanted to take with me were there. Now the lorries were full, my cousins were on board, my sister, all my family. And this woman stood behind me, alone. Her husband and baby were still in the block. Now an SS man was closing the gate. Schwarzhuber remained at the lectern sorting the index cards.

I stood at attention before him, "Doctor Schwarzhuber, here is my cousin. She has a baby and her husband is also a cousin of mine. Can I take them with me?"

"Yes," he said, "be quick, be very quick!" I dashed back with her into the block. I was barely able to leave the block again for people clinging to me and pleading with me to take them. I wanted to take the entire block – the entire camp – but it wasn't possible. We fetched her husband and baby and left. The gate was closed behind us; we were the last. Relief flooded over me. I was sitting in the lorry. I was happy that my wife, my sister and cousins were with me, that we had got out alive.

We were taken to Auschwitz Main Camp where we remained for a few days. My brother Erich was also there, in block 11. A few weeks previously they had promised him release under the condition that he be sterilised.[73] We were loaded into wagons in Auschwitz Main Camp. The wagons were crammed full. We were shunted onto a siding. We said to ourselves, "Wait, you'll see, this evening we'll be gassed." We could not get out as the SS had bolted the doors from the outside. We stood in these wagons practically the whole afternoon. Those people remaining in the Gypsy Camp who were still fairly fit climbed up onto the roofs of the blocks. We talked to them through the slits in the wagons. We took leave of one another.[74] We didn't know that they ... All those remaining in the camp, were to be gassed. All were gassed. Prisoners told us this after we had arrived in Ravensbrück from Auschwitz.[75]

Late in the evening the locomotive was coupled up. The train departed. We were moving. The train halted once more at Auschwitz station then departed. We were entrained without provisions. We were a whole day travelling but I cannot be more precise. We repeatedly stopped and waited at stations. It was still light when we arrived. We were in Ravensbrück.[76] On arrival we men were separated from the women and children. My wife, my sister and my brother's wife were imprisoned in the women's camp. My wife was pregnant. She clung to me but the SS forced us apart: "Get on!"

Ravensbrück

We men were imprisoned in the men's camp of Ravensbrück concentration camp.[77] There was only a wall separating the men's and women's camp. In the evenings we talked to each other from one side of the wall to the other, but in our own language. The SS couldn't understand what we said. There were not many blocks in the men's camp, perhaps five. There was also a kitchen, situated lengthwise, and an infirmary block. In comparison with the women's camp there were not many male prisoners. They were mainly employed as craftsmen.[78] We also passed ourselves off as craftsmen; we were handy as carpenters and could do practically everything. We joined the carpenters and gained access to the women's camp where we fitted doors and windows in the new blocks. We also spoke to our women. This had to be done in a matter of seconds, swiftly, in passing. We were guarded very closely. Once, my wife came to the window where I was working. The situation was dramatic. I had to forcibly prevent her from entering through the window. If the SS had seen this they would have shot us on the spot. My wife died in Ravensbrück on Christmas Eve 1944. Our child had died at birth three days before. I never saw our child. A sintezza told me at the wall that my wife and child had died. Naturally I was not officially informed.

My sister Maria was transported from Ravensbrück to Wittenberge concentration camp.[79] Here she worked as forced labour. During an air raid, when the electricity was

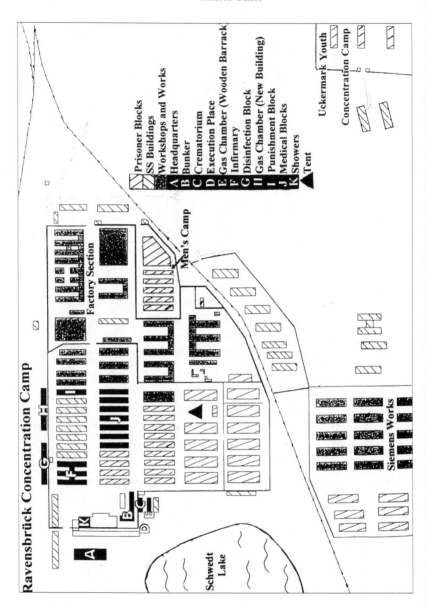

Plan of Ravensbrück concentration camp.

turned off, she escaped with a Polish female prisoner. On reaching the woods they heard a rustling behind them and were confronted by a male escapee who directed them on their way. They travelled by night exchanging their striped prisoner uniform for clothes they came across on washing lines. Maria returned home safely where she remained undiscovered until the end of the war.

Five of us men were employed in the building-supplies yard where we had to hand out the tools. One day we had to leave the camp to fell wood and cut it into metre lengths.[80] This was close to the camp, directly behind the watchtower. The wood was a little hilly. There was a dug-out, I presume for the guards, in the case of an air raid. The bunker was open on two sides. You could go below and shelter. The day before we had 'organised' a few potatoes and had taken them with us to the wood. The SS men sat apart smoking and there was a watchtower with a guard nearby. I had 'organised' a sort of jam can.

"I'm going to cook the potatoes," I told the others and, as I entered the bunker, I asked a seventeen-year-old, a Hungarian Gypsy from Austria,[81] "keep watch while I make a fire." We made a tiny fire so that it made no smoke, constantly stoking it. Entirely unexpectedly, an SS man came from the other direction and stood before me.

"What's going on?" He kicked the can and the potatoes spilled out. "Number?" He wrote down my number and the lad's number. "Report this evening!"

As I came out of the bunker I saw a prisoner with an SS man behind him with a revolver in his hand on their way to the watchtower. The SS man grabbed the prisoner's cap from behind and threw it over the camp fence. The prisoner turned round. "Fetch your cap!" the SS man ordered him. I was perhaps thirty or forty metres away. The prisoner didn't want to. The SS man gave him a shove with his revolver, "Go, fetch your cap!" He walked to the cap, had not completely bent down when the SS man shot him in the back of the head. He lay there: shot "while attempting to escape".

Walter Winter's letter to his parents from Ravensbrück.

In the meantime, our SS man had written down my number and had joined the other SS man. I thought, "When this murderer now learns about the potatoes he will probably kill me too." But this didn't happen. We marched back to the camp in the evening, fell in and were counted. Following the count my number was called out and that of the lad.

"Step forward!"

Felled tree trunks with roots lay at the camp entrance. These were thick tree trunks! The others were allowed to fall out. We had to go to the entrance. "So, each of you grab a trunk and hold it above your head! And stand at the front by the fence!" We had to stand in the off-limits zone directly adjacent to the electrified perimeter fence holding these tree trunks. To the left of us was the Block Commanders' room with windows overlooking the perimeter fence.

I must say, at this time I was in a bad way. We stood there, the lad to my left. It was evening and already dark. The others had marched in at 5pm and been fed. We were still standing there at half past ten. We had been holdings those logs for five and a half hours.

The lad said, "I'm all in! I'm all in!"

The window of the Block Commanders' room was perhaps ten or twelve metres away. The Block Commander saw my mouth moving. I continuously encouraged the boy, "Hold on to me, lean on me!"

He did this but all the same, "I'm all in! I'm all in! I'm going to let myself fall against the wire."

"No," I said, "No, you don't. Hold on, hold on, they'll call us soon. Hold on a little longer!" We held out but the lad really was at the end of his tether.

My brother suffered with us. Sometimes, it was more difficult being together with brothers, with family, than being alone. It was sometimes advantageous and sometimes not. My brother stood behind our block and looked across to us. He crept behind the kitchen block and spoke to us,

"I've put your food aside for you." Our Block Senior was

a political prisoner.

My brother told him, "The two are still outside…"

He said, "We'll put the food aside for them." He kept the leftovers for us both. At eleven o'clock they let us in. From five to eleven we had to stand there each holding a tree trunk on our heads. It must have weighed 15–20 kilos. I was so sorry for the lad. Had he been alone he would have fallen on the wire and been electrocuted. We entered the block and the Block Senior gave us the food. There was five litres for me and five litres for the lad, a sort of noodles, dog food. I couldn't lie down in the night, couldn't die, couldn't live, I was so bloated. Five litres! We survived the ordeal.

Hunger

When we were working in the building-supplies yard at Ravensbrück, there was a dog pound nearby.[82] An SS man was cooking lovely food for the dogs. It smelled so good! Noodles and ribbon vermicelli with horsemeat. Although, strictly speaking, I don't eat horsemeat,[83] I would have eaten it with pleasure. I was a non-smoker and my brother wasn't a heavy smoker. The SS man was cooking in a large field-kitchen. I was stacking planks at the time.

I called to him, "Hello!"

He looked across at me, "What's up?"

"I'm a non-smoker," I said, "I have cigarettes. Could we have some of the dog food?"

"Well," he considered this, thought it over, muttered to himself. "How many cigarettes do you have, then?"

"Two, and my brother has two," I answered.

"OK, bring them here!"

"I can't. If I come to you now and I'm seen by someone I'll be shot straight away." There was a watchtower and railway lines nearby.

"Ach, don't worry. Come here!" There was a barbed-wire fence between us, not electrified. The ground was white sand. He said, "I'll set it down here for you!" He couldn't bring it to us. "Leave the cigarettes here." Well, he put down a bowl, I scrambled under the wire, left the cigarettes and came back like the clappers. We now had this bowl for five men. That tasted good! That tasted so good! Two days later I traded socks

I had 'organised'. We got the same again. Twice and then that was the end of it.

On another occasion we 'organised' potatoes. That was funny. Today this would belong to a comedian's act. The building-supplies yard stood directly opposite the camp entrance on the other side of the road. We were in the building site. Five wagons of potatoes stood on the tracks. Adjacent to the entrance to the men's camp was an entrance to the women's camp. The potatoes were loaded onto wheelbarrows, one after the other. When a wheelbarrow was full it was pushed round to the depot in the women's camp, or sometimes to us in the men's camp. It was fifty metres from the wagons to us in the building-supplies yard and to the dog pound. Among us was a middle-aged man from Munich, Thomas Höllenreiner.[84] He was a card. I was always happy when I was with him. He cheered me up.

He said to me in his Bavarian dialect, "The potatoes there, we'll take a barrow full."

"Thomas, we won't get away with it alive," I said, for there was a watchtower directly behind the wagons and another on the other side of the road. The SS men were standing in a circle smoking and talking. There were ten men with wheelbarrows. To get to them we would have to cross the road and stand at the end of the queue.

Thomas said, "Look here. You take the wheelbarrow and I'll put a potato sack over my arm and take hold of the shaft." There were always two men to push a barrow.

"Thomas, this could mean our death," I said.

"Ach, lad, not us, no, no, no!"

"OK. I'm with you!"

We took a wheelbarrow from the building site, threw a sack over it and he threw a sack over his arm and joined the end of the line.

It wasn't that difficult. The SS men didn't notice us. The lads in the wagons threw the potatoes into the barrows. When one barrow was full the next was brought up.

"Next!" It was our turn. They filled the barrow. We moved off.

I said, "Thomas, watch, now comes a shot from above when we leave in this direction."

"No, lad, don't look round! Walk straight ahead!" That was the opposite direction to the others. I thought, "Now, now, now ..." Over the road, straight ahead, to the building site. No one followed, no one noticed. We had the potatoes. We tipped them out behind the pile of planks. We had potatoes for the next few days. We laughed afterwards, having got the better of the SS.

Oranienburg-Sachsenhausen

In the meantime my brother had been sterilised together with four other men. They were the first. My eldest cousin was also sterilised. That was in Ravensbrück, not Auschwitz.[85] Then we heard that the next were in line. This Thomas Höllenreiner,[86] a forty-five-year-old from Munich, also a Sinto, said to me, "Walter, listen, we'll wait until last. Who knows what will happen in the meantime." Well, we were always a little... When, after a few days, these men returned, the next five had to report. We always managed not to be in the next group of five.

Then we suddenly heard, "All fall in!" We were transferred from Ravensbrück to Oranienburg-Sachsenhausen[87] in open wagons. It was cold, so cold that we almost froze alive.

We had to walk from Oranienburg railway station, from sidings, to Sachsenhausen concentration camp. The inscription above the main gate again read, *Arbeit macht frei*. We had to enter the Gestapo office one at a time and were individually searched. We had smuggled a watch and several diamonds out of Auschwitz. We thought, "Wait, they can still be of value to us." The SS hadn't told us where we were being sent.

My brother had to enter first.

"Have you brought anything of value with you?" They knew that there were plenty of valuables in Auschwitz.

"Yes, a watch."

"And what else?"

"Here, I also have some diamonds." They would have

98

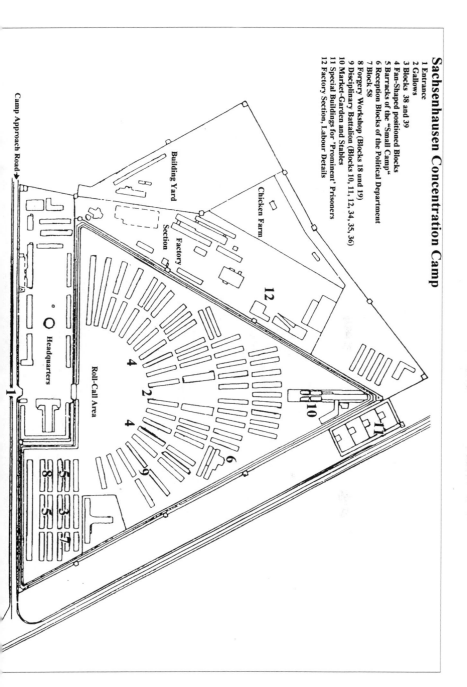

Sachsenhausen Concentration Camp

1 Entrance
2 Gallows
3 Blocks 38 and 39
4 Fan-Shaped positioned Blocks
5 Barracks of the "Small Camp"
6 Reception Blocks of the Political Department
7 Block 58
8 Forgery Workshop (Blocks 18 und 19)
9 Disciplinary Battalion (Blocks 10, 11, 12, 34, 35, 36)
10 Market-Garden and Stables
11 Special Buildings for 'Prominent' Prisoners
12 Factory Section, Labour Details

Camp Approach Road

Building Yard

Chicken Farm

Factory Section

Headquarters

Roll-Call Area

Plan of Sachsenhausen concentration camp.

99

searched him anyway. You had to lay everything upon a blue velvet cloth.

When it was my turn I handed over only the watch.

Leaving this office, we entered through the main gate again and then turned right. Here were numerous blocks in one of which we remained for several days. It was only afterwards that I saw the death blocks with gallows behind sectioned off by a wooden gate. Shootings also took place. My brother Erich remained in this initial block while I was moved. We were separated for the first time. I was transferred to block 33.[88] Here I rapidly lost weight. I have a large nose anyway and it looked even longer with the bones protruding. Had I remained there another four or six weeks I would have been dead.

But we didn't remain long in Sachsenhausen. During this time we again worked in the woods, the Hungarian lad too. Luckily we were together in the same block again. We had to cut tree trunks into metre lengths. As in Ravensbrück, the dog pound for the SS dog squadron was in the woods. The dogs were being fed while we cut wood.

I said, "Hell! You know what? I'll ask the old man there." An elderly SS man had just entered the kennels and was feeding the dogs. I said, "We have cigarettes." The lad didn't smoke either. "Could you give us a dog biscuit? Then you can have our cigarettes."

He remained standing in the doorway so that he could not be seen by the other SS men, "Yes, but you'll have to fetch it from the pound yourselves."

"OK. But keep the dogs in check!"

"Yes, OK."

When these dogs saw us cutting wood or when we moved a little to the side they stuck their fangs through the wire. They were specially trained against people in striped, prisoner clothing. On our side of the dog pound was a hatch that opened outwards; you could lift this flap. The dogs entered and left through this.

I asked, "What do we do now?"

"Yes," asked the lad, "how do we get the biscuits out? We can't reach them with a stick."

First, we had to throw the cigarettes into the pound. The SS man picked these up. Then he took some dog biscuits and, from the door, threw them into the middle of the cage instead of by the wire.

I said, "Now we've lost our cigarettes and the biscuits are lying there. Dog biscuits! Listen, we'll do this: I'll lift up the flap and enter while you take hold of my legs. As soon as you see a dog, pull me out and I'll push backwards with my arms." We lifted the flap, the SS man called the dogs to him, but just as I had the biscuits in my hands the dogs advanced on me. I yelled, "Pull!" I managed to get only one biscuit; just as the flap fell shut the dogs had their fangs in the wire.

I now had the biscuit in my hand and wanted to break it in two but I couldn't because it was so hard. It contained bone. Two more biscuits lay in the cage. I told the Hungarian lad, "We must have them as well. We'll take them and soften them up back in camp." We got nothing to eat in the morning, only a mug of water. You couldn't call it coffee. In the evening, when we marched back, we got a thin slice of bread. That was the entire day's ration. "We'll soften up the biscuits. But how do we get them? The dogs will tear us apart. Listen, we'll swap over. You're lighter than me, you enter the cage."

I said to the SS man, "Sling the biscuits a little further towards us!"

He wouldn't do this. "No! If you want them, then fetch them out."

"All right, then call the dogs back." This he did. Exactly like the first time: the flap up, the lad in, me pushing him. He had just got the biscuits in his hand when the dogs were again in the door. I pulled him back, he hurt his arm. We couldn't eat the biscuits. We couldn't bite into them, couldn't soften them.

Once, a skinned horse hung on the gallows for the dogs. I

said, "You know what? Such a good piece of meat, if we could just get at it! It would be something we could eat."

"Yes! I'll get it," the lad said.

"You can't go there," I told him. The horse hung directly before a kitchen window. "Don't go past the window. Go underneath. Bend down or crawl." He crawled but didn't get to the horse. However, before it lay a pile of kitchen waste. There was white cabbage, red cabbage, everything imaginable. When, from my cover behind the block, I saw the cook come out a number of times I beckoned to the lad, "Come back, come back now!" Well, he waited for the right moment and crawled to the pile of waste. He grabbed hold of a red cabbage lying there and his fingers sank in. It was rotten. He crawled back with this cabbage. It was a large head which we pared back and pared back. What remained was the size of a tennis ball. We didn't throw away the rotten leaves. We took one of the cans lying near this kitchen waste and placed the cabbage leaves in this with a little water and made a tiny fire with small strips of wood. Smoke would have given us away. We had matches for such occasions. We shared this, each of us receiving a few leaves.

One afternoon the foreman of the woodcutting detail came to us.

"Come in lads! Have a bowl of soup!"

"Oh! Soup?" All the woodcutters entered the block. He shared out the soup. We had no bowls, not having considered such a thing. Well, everyone got soup. From mugs. We got half a mug each. That was good!

I asked, "What meat was that made with?"

"Well, that was dog."

"What?" He had killed and cooked the guard's dog. We didn't get any of the meat but the soup was sheer poetry, that hot soup was sheer poetry.

Air Raid

In Sachsenhausen we were occupied with various kinds of work. One day we were working outside the camp. There was a major attack, an air raid. Although the camp was not the target of this attack, it came within its range. All labour details were ordered back to the camp. The bombs started to fall. The SS took cover and so did we. The camp perimeter wall was roughly fifty metres away. We were near a road where telephone poles were piled. Normally, you wouldn't have been able to get beneath them but I managed to get my head beneath a pole at right angles to the pile. My lower half remained exposed. A bomb fell. And what a bomb! It formed a crater ten metres wide not far away from us but we were spared. Suddenly, I felt heat between the legs. I lay on my stomach, head and arms under the pole. I scrambled out and saw an incendiary bomb ablaze directly behind me. Twenty centimetres more and the fragment would have hit my back; it now lay between my legs.

I saw a crater and said to the Hungarian lad, "Come on! Get into the crater! Another bomb won't fall there." I learnt that in the navy. We got into the crater, under an oak tree that had been toppled. We crawled beneath this tree. I said, "The incendiary bombs are no danger to us here. We must get to the wall, they won't drop them on the camp." All the incendiary bombs and other bombs fell on the factory situated close by. We ran to the wall where we felt relatively safe.

When the bombers had left we had to fall in. We were to

march back to the camp. But a new wave of bombers arrived overhead. To the left was a field, an open field of potatoes. I lay there with my nose in the earth, there was nowhere else to hide. I lay there, the lad too, until all the bombs had fallen. I must say, in all honesty, that I prayed for my life. Well, I lay with my face directly on a potato. I opened my eyes and thought, "Take it with you." I took two large potatoes. I didn't know where I could hide them. I hid one under my left armpit, the other under the right. If you looked suspicious when you marched back into camp you were immediately called out. On either side of the entrance gate stood five SS men scrutinising the column. "Come out!" That was your death sentence, they called that "looting". We marched into the camp and fortunately I avoided their suspicion. They had already called out some before me and then several behind me. We fell in on the roll-call area. There we met with a body hanging from the mast bearing a sign, "I have looted!"

I returned to my block, block 33. There was a cylindrical iron stove in the block. Each individual 'organised' what he could. We cooked this on the stove. We placed our metal pots on the stove one after the other. Each of us waited our turn. But we didn't have any proper fuel. Each block had only a little coal. That was all. Those that got to the stove first were fortunate. When my turn came I was able only to place my pot on the edge. It started to steam a little but not to cook. I had cleaned the potatoes before placing them in the pot. Then it was ten o'clock curfew when we had to be in our bunks. The SS entered the blocks to check. I had to remove my pot from the stove. I ate the slightly warm potatoes in my bunk. At least I had something.

Service at the Front

There were further air raids. A few days later, we had to fall in and we were given the order, "Former Wehrmacht soldiers, step forward!" There were perhaps 150 men remaining. We had to report to the infirmary block. Here we were clothed as SS men and given food: field rations of bread, 500 grams of margarine and jam. My brother Erich and I kept ourselves under control. We didn't eat everything immediately. When we were kitted out I saw the chance of 'freedom' and thought, "Now. This is the moment when you're out and free." Our watches were returned to us. We had to report, individually, to headquarters. There lay a cloth full of diamonds. The Commandant[89] said, "Pick out your belongings." I took my watch. My brother took his watch and two diamonds roughly the size of those he had brought with him. They were beautiful stones.

The next day we had to march to the station where we were loaded into wagons. We marched out of the camp at 8am on 13 April 1945. I shall never forget that moment! There was a clock on the entrance gate and at precisely eight o'clock the barrier was lowered behind us. We were on the outside. I said to Erich, "You know what? This is our salvation."

We were loaded onto wagons, as soldiers. Then the train waited in a siding. We had uniforms but no papers, no belts, no steel helmets, no weapons. We saw a grocer's shop at the bottom of the embankment. We had to wait the entire afternoon with the grocer's shop in sight. It was now or never. I went to the duty officer and asked, "Excuse me, there's a grocer's shop below. Can we go and buy something?" We had some money, I no longer remember how we had come by it. Anyway, we took two men with us and bought what we could. No SS man accompanied us. They merely stood above observing us. We descended the embankment and crossed the road.

The train left shortly thereafter. It stopped again in a pine wood. Nearby was a small farm; we sat at the edge of the wood. Here we received our weapons. Suddenly a detachment arrived and dug a pit. What was going on? We realised that someone was going to be shot. Two soldiers hadn't reported back from leave, that was 'desertion'. I heard that they had been arrested at home. One had hanged himself, the other was to be shot in our presence, purposely in our presence, as intimidation. Then they arrived, an officer with two soldiers and the so-called 'delinquent'. The 'delinquent' had to stand on top of the mound of dug-out sand. The officer, a second lieutenant, read him his sentence. Then he ordered the two soldiers to take aim. "Strip to the waist! Fire!"

When they took aim, the lad, he was a young lad, said, "Comrades, aim well!" He was a brave lad.

The second lieutenant walked to the pit, looked to see if he was dead, gave him a shot in the head and ordered the pit to be filled in. He had to pass through the group of us because we were sitting scattered about. He said, "I had no other choice!" We made no comment. He was a young lad himself, twenty-one or twenty-two years old. His conscience troubled him and he mumbled to himself, "I only carried out my orders." He was too shaken to know what to say. He was an ordinary army officer. It happened in our presence as we sat or lay there. That was our first shock.

We were a special unit: Dirlewanger.[90] We found ourselves in the trenches on the Oder-Neisse Line. We were also under surveillance; I didn't realise this at first. A young snot was positioned behind me with a machine gun, not next to me in the trench but above in the field. The Russians were on the opposite bank of the Neisse. The Neisse is not a wide river. The Russians had a gramophone with a horn which they placed on the dyke. They played music. The SS shot at them. A Russian called over, "Comrade, don't shoot! Sleep!"

Five of us deserted, my cousin among them. They swam across to the Russians and surrendered. They were a shock troop whose task it was to take prisoners. The next day the Russians called out our names over loudspeakers from the other side of the embankment. There must have been a road there. You could see the tops of apple trees. The loudspeaker van drove along this road and the lads called out our names telling us we should come over, we would be welcomed. The Russians knew we had been in concentration camps, they knew everything.

The next day the Russians attacked. It appeared that three Russians were crossing the river. Everyone looked the same in uniform. I sprang out of the trench. I thought, "Do something before the Russians do something to you!" I had to protect my own life! But I didn't squeeze the trigger, I did nothing, I simply called, "Halt!" They didn't remain where they were. One called out in German, "Hey, it's me!" They were two of our lads with a captive Russian between them. I had a hand grenade in my hand. That was will power! To this day I can't understand how the SS were able to shoot people in the camps like animals. These SS men, their faces… When I remember how they shot the young lad on the side of the drainage ditch of the Gypsy Camp … and the one who shot and killed the woman through the wall of the block. I have told you of these killings. That must have been a real delight, a pleasure for them. At home, I couldn't even kill a chicken. When my father said, "Kill it, chop off its head!" I was unable to. But Plagge, Palitzsch and all the others, they sneered and they laughed so strangely… the way they persecuted the people, including the children.

Encircled Seven Times

One afternoon, tanks advanced on us. The tanks came up through a fairly wide depression. A runner came to me and said, "Listen, there's a fuse on the bridge. Blow up the bridge!" A Russian tank was positioned fifty metres from this bridge. I would have had to approach over open ground, the Russians would have clearly seen me and mown me down. I thought, "Don't be crazy and get yourself killed in the last minute!" I took off. There was a trench to the left full of holes and dead bodies. I leapt over them and ran towards the trees ahead. An infantry officer was standing there with a revolver in his hand, "Back! Back! Back!" No one took any notice of him, but passed him by and left him standing there. We ran from the Russians but we always reported back to our unit. They sent us back to the front again, back to the trenches. The SS caught us; they were standing on the road.

One of our number, a Sinto, had been wounded in the leg and could no longer walk. My brother and I were supporting him. We thought, "We'll take him to the field hospital." SS men with a machine gun were standing in front of the hospital. "Back!" they ordered us.

"He's wounded!" we replied.

At that moment a motorcyclist with sidecar arrived. "Sit him in!"

We sat him in the sidecar then they sent us back. "Straight back to the trenches!"

We didn't go back to the trenches as the Russians had

taken them. In the evening the SS tried to drive us back into the trenches yet again.

"Heavens, what do we do now?" my brother asked. We had to return to the trenches. You couldn't do a runner. We returned to our position and I trod on something soft. I thought, "What's that?" It was pitch-black. I had fallen into a trench and was standing on a dead soldier. I felt his face and jumped out in fright.

It was the same the next day. You wanted to desert but you couldn't escape. Just when you thought, "We've dodged those sentries!" yet other SS men stood before you and turned you back. Then we formed a squad of ten to thirteen men, all Sinti. My brother Erich led us. We reached a small village but they caught us again.

We were told, "We must take this village. Some of our comrades are trapped there." Evening. Night. Waiting. We were 300 men and a tank. We attacked, we advanced through the village and the Russians retreated. Then we heard the lads calling from the cellars, "Comrades, take us with you!" No one had paid them any heed.

The next day the Russians attacked again. We were continuously encircled. We were encircled seven times. During one encirclement the Russians left everything: horses and wagons, mortars. They advanced quickly. Suddenly my brother said, "I've been hit!" We took cover behind a woodpile. I looked under his coat. We had discarded the SS jackets and had taken jackets from dead soldiers: I had an infantry jacket and my brother an air force jacket. He had wanted to take a cap from one and had been about to place it on his head when he saw that half the brains were still inside. I lifted his jacket and saw he had been hit by shrapnel. It hadn't entered his body, there was merely a red spot. I said, "It's nothing!" As I replaced his jacket I heard something behind me. I looked round and saw a Russian with a knife in his hand. A young lad, perhaps seventeen. His face was white as chalk. My brother and I had left our weapons by the woodpile. I grabbed my weapon and the Russian dropped his knife.

"Don't! Comrade!" I said, "*Dawai!*" That means, "Scram!" He turned and was about to run when an SS man came out of the bushes.

"What's this? Come here!" He took the lad a short distance away and we heard two shots...

Awake at often nights I often thought, "Man, how have you managed to survive all this?" To be sure, I was twenty-three or twenty-four. We were, of course, athletic. Today when I go out and it's cold I immediately start to freeze. For the time we were in Auschwitz we had only canvas material to wear and and the winter was cold.

Journey Home

The war ended in May 1945. We were on the River Spree. We crossed over in an inflatable dinghy. There must have been 200 to 300 soldiers on the riverbank, from all three services: army, navy, air force. There was a fight for the boat as only three or four men could get in at one time. We got across and marched on. We were shot at while crossing a road. We were encircled again. Here I received a bullet wound. It entered one shoulder and lodged in the other. I could no longer move my body. I lay three days in a wagon. We rested at farms at night, slept with the tractor. We were the wounded. We were two days underway and on the third day were encircled by the Russians again.

I said to Erich, "You know what you should do? Put your arm in a sling." The idea was for him to pass himself off as one of the wounded.

We had some cunning people among us. One, a sergeant – I remember it to this day – sat on a white horse. The other officers had thrown their uniforms away. He negotiated with a Russian in a tank. I couldn't understand what they said.

The sergeant returned and raged: "Comrades, shall we surrender? Or shall we fight on?"

Some shouted, "Let us fight!"

The older soldiers were for surrendering. We too, naturally. They unhorsed this sergeant: "Tell them we surrender!" We surrendered, threw our weapons in a heap. Then the Russians came and demanded our watches but my brother and I had hidden ours. We had to repeatedly raise our arms, raise our shirtsleeves. One Russian had hung an alarm clock round his neck on a string and both his arms were covered in watches. He couldn't believe we didn't have a watch!

Then we were told, "The wounded on this side, onto the lorries. They come with us. All the others who are able to walk, on the other side. The day after tomorrow they go home." Again, we were on our way. In the first town the hospital was overflowing but we were admitted to the hospital in Luckenwalde, south of Berlin. The following day a captive SS man operated on me. There was no anaesthetic; I felt everything. I was a little groggy but nevertheless wriggled like an eel.

Erich had to assist. He told this SS man, "I'll kill you if anything happens to my brother."

He answered, "I'll do my best!"

I lay there eight days. Then we met a cousin whose family lived in Luckenwalde. They had been stuck there the entire war with their circus. This cousin spoke to the officer and he discharged me. A train was leaving for Berlin. We spoke to the station manager.

"Yes, board the train!"

I had the address in Berlin of a woman who had been in our block in Auschwitz. We made such arrangements: "Should we get out, we'll meet there and there!" I remembered it was Alexanderplatz. We tried to find it. There was only rubble; there were no road signs left. We asked a woman who was clearing rubble with a bucket and brush, "Yes, round the corner here!" There was nothing left of Alexanderplatz that could be recognised. Had we walked further we wouldn't have found it. From Berlin we travelled further on foot. I was running a temperature of 39-40 degrees Celsius. We walked thirty or forty kilometres a day. We stopped in the evenings and asked if we could sleep somewhere or other. Once we were told, "Yes, here," by the former Ortsgruppenleiter.[91] "Of course you may."

We got our next train in Hannover: destination Bremen. We ran along the lines into the station. The signalman cursed us. There was no passenger train for Germans but there was one for Americans. We looked into the carriages. The Americans were on board sleeping. The train was to depart early the next morning. We said, "You know what? We'll board and lie down too." We lay down and covered ourselves. There were enough blankets. In Bremen we removed the blankets and got off. We continued walking until we came to Delmenhorst in the district of Oldenburg. Here the bridges had also been destroyed. On the other side of Delmenhorst we met a farmer on a tractor pulling a milk cart.

We asked him, "Can you give us a lift."

"Yes, jump up!" He took us as far as Großenkneten. From there we continued on foot again.

Shortly before Wildeshausen we met a lorry. I said, "He must give us a lift!" We waved him down and who should it turn out to be? An acquaintance. A haulage contractor from Cloppenburg! Before the war we had driven for him when he required a driver.

"Man, where have you come from? Jump up!" He took us to Cloppenburg.

When we arrived home my grandmother was speechless. She said, "You're dead."

"How come?"

"We were told they had hanged you."

"Well, here we are." She couldn't believe her eyes. Of course we asked, "Where are our parents?" They were in Lohne, already travelling with the business. An ex-soldier, from Lohne, was passing and he knew my grandparents.

"Are you going to Lohne?" we asked him.

"Yes."

"Can you take a message?"

"Yes, of course!" I wrote a quick note and gave it to him. Then my father arrived with the horse and wagon. He must have driven like the wind. My parents had parked the vehicles to the rear of the *Schutzenhof*,[92] some distance outside the village. My mother was sitting at the table outside. Our dog, which we had reared, had not seen us for over two years. He was sitting about a hundred metres away but he recognised us immediately. He ran and jumped up at us! And my mother ... we were home.

PART THREE

The Post-War Period and Remembrance

Afterwards

At mobilisation in 1939 we had packed everything and travelled to Cloppenburg. My father bought a house, a small thatched cottage. It was taken from us during the war and not paid for. It was simply taken from us. When we returned from the concentration camps it was returned to us. We forced them to return it. They weren't prepared to return it of their own accord.

The lads with whom we had gone to school and played football were now local authority civil servants. They knew precisely who we were. Nevertheless, they wanted to register my brother Erich and myself as being stateless.

Walter Winter, winter 1945.

"Identity card?" demanded one of them as he filled out the form and came to the box for nationality. "I have to write 'stateless'," he explained.

I was flabbergasted. Did we make a stink! I said, "Just a minute! You're not going to write that! Don't you dare write that." I addressed him in the familiar 'du' form;[93] we had been at school together, we had been good friends. "Don't you dare write 'stateless'! There'll be trouble if you do!" I said to him, "Didn't we go to school together? Didn't we play football together?"

"Yes."

"And didn't we used to live here? Didn't we grow up here?"

"Yes."

"And you want to write 'stateless'! Don't you dare! We were born here!" I brought my fist down on the table with a loud bang. Our shouted protests were so loud that all the doors along the corridor were opened. There was a proper argy-bargy!

"All right," he said, "all right, all right!" I could have knocked his head off there and then. He then wrote 'German'. Apparently, they had been instructed not to register us Sinti as German. I don't know for sure but I assume they had such an order. How otherwise did he come to have the idea?

It was the same with the house. We didn't even demand the rent from the man who had lived there. He wasn't responsible. Nevertheless, had we wanted, we could have demanded the two and a half years' rent. They officially returned our house to us. We then sold it. We exchanged it for a Hanomag towing vehicle owned by a horse dealer. My father said, "Give me the vehicle and you get the house." The vehicle was of more value to us. It was like this: after we returned, our parents, my brother-in-law, Erich and I were in Vechta. What were we to do? My father had sold the shooting gallery at the end of the war. At that time he knew nothing of

Walter Winter, in the circus arena of Circus Winter and Sons, prior to the 1948 currency reform.

our whereabouts, he had no news of us and we had lost contact with one another. Anyway, we decided, "Let's establish a circus!" My father knew a lot about the business. "We'll establish a circus. We'll begin with a variety act and then when we've earned a few pence we'll buy animals." We were not allowed to start our variety show before being denazified![94] I went to the English commander and told him our story. Nevertheless, we still had to be denazified! It was a formality but we had to give all our personal details and show our identity cards.

One year later, we were in Vechta again. The old mayor, the Nazi, was still in office. In the meantime, we had horses, we were running our circus and had had a circus tent made for us. We needed feed for the horses. My brother and I went to the authorities to acquire ration coupons.[95] This mayor said he wasn't authorised to do this and also wasn't prepared to. Suddenly, he said, "Just a moment, I'll make a telephone call." He went into the next room and telephoned. Immediately, an Englishman entered the room: an officer with a riding crop under his arm. He spoke to the mayor in German. He told us, "Shut up!" and held the riding crop as though he was about to hit us with it. We wanted to explain that we needed feed coupons but he didn't give us the chance; he threw us out as though we were dogs.

In the period immediately after the war you were happy simply to be home and to have survived. You said to yourself, "So, now you must see that you get back on your feet." The business with the circus wasn't easy. Then came the currency reform.[96] We were in Schleswig-Holstein, in Itzehoe. Nobody came to the circus. Nor in Pinneberg. We tried everywhere. In Wedel town centre we once again earned good money with the circus but after that there was no business, no more customers, no one anymore. After the currency reform people held onto their money. We said to ourselves, my father, my brother and I, "It's financially very bad. If it continues like this we'll be destitute. Let's take up the fairground business again." My father sold everything, the horses, the business, the circus tent, anything we no longer needed. He bought a fairground caterpillar ride with the proceeds. My brother stayed with my father and they earned their living with the caterpillar ride but three men were too many for this business, let alone three families. I built an ice-cream stall and became independent; we have remained in the fairground business ever since.

Immediately after the war you did not think that much about the Nazi period and the camps. You were simply glad to have survived. You built a new life. The years passed by. It is only in the last twenty years, when things have become a little more settled, that the memories have returned and I have had to come to terms with what I experienced under the Nazis. The more I think about my suffering the more hate I feel.

I have revisited the camps. In 1986 my wife Marion and I took a coach journey to Auschwitz, and we revisited Oranienburg-Sachsenhausen from Berlin. We spent three hours there and saw everything. We also visited Ravensbrück. I looked round at the rear where the crematorium once stood because my first wife and our child died there. We were not officially married at a registry office but in accordance with Sinti custom.

In 1986, while on a three-week holiday with my wife Marion in Sri Lanka, I ran into an SS man. We lay next to him on the beach. He came from our area, near Wilhelmshaven. We got into conversation. I told him I had been in the navy. I didn't mention the camps. Then I noticed how he looked at the number on my arm. I saw how, in the last week of the holiday, this preyed on his mind.

By this time we were on 'du' terms as we had often sat together, and he said, "Hey, Walter, I must ask you something."

"Fire away!"

"I saw the number on your arm. Is that from a concentration camp?"

"Yes," I told him.

"I was in the SS. I was in a tank division." I knew of such Waffen SS tank divisions.[97] "And when I say I had nothing to do with these camps, you can believe me." I let him talk. He asked me which camp I had been in. I do believe he wasn't involved but when I hear 'SS' I feel an immediate hostility. He talked and talked about the war and I honestly believed he had nothing to do with the camps. Nevertheless, for me... The fact that he was in the SS ... He also related where they had been and which battles they had fought. We left it at that. I kept my feelings to myself. We flew back to Germany. He flew back with us. Then he said, "You must come and visit me!" I assume this was his conscience pricking him. "You can stay with me on holiday if you want. Free of charge." He owned two hotels, one at Jadebusen, and the other on the North Sea. He wrote me a Christmas card. He wrote to me a few more times but I didn't reply. The word 'SS' alone was enough for me. I noticed how he had looked at my arm. I sensed that. The majority say nothing. They know what the number is. They know exactly what it is.

In 1991 we were on holiday on the island of Gran Canaria where we met a retired officer. He was a nice guy. He must have been sixty or sixty-five years old.

He asked me, "What's that?"

I answered, "You know perfectly well what it is!"

"No."

"It's an Auschwitz number!" I said.

"Ah so," he replied.

That was all. He didn't ask any further; that was that. Hell, you can't always be wearing a plaster on your arm! I won't do that!

I was a soldier myself and saw enough dead soldiers. Perhaps it helped somewhat in the camps to have acquired an understanding of what death was in the war. But you saw so many dead in the camps, all murdered. I had to work a day in the crematorium myself, I was caught for a day, I had no choice. In books you read: it was like this, and this. The authors always write that so and so many people were murdered and that the people were maltreated. That is correct, that is all true, but you don't read about the feelings, the constant fear. There are things that people cannot begin to comprehend. Yet I remember everything.

Other people suffered in the war. Soldiers too, but they had weapons and were free. When there was an air raid, they could take shelter. They could fight against the enemy they faced. We in the camps were forced to accept everything; we were completely powerless. Then this humiliation because of your so-called 'racial origin'. Is this my fault? Is this the

Walter Winter, 2003.

fault of my parents? And that is what I fear, that these right-wing extremists, these Nazis, will get the upper hand once again. This makes me uneasy. This book is my statement of opposition. No Sinto, no individual, should ever have to suffer what we suffered.

Endnotes

1. Horsemeat is taboo within traditional Sinti culture.
2. In the early 1960s West Germany (FRG) experienced its greatest economic boom (Wirtschaftswunder) after World War II. Turks were invited, as guest workers (Gastarbeiter), to make up for the shortage of manpower. They were regarded as guests and it was not anticipated that they would stay once their services were no longer required. They did, however, remain and are now the largest immigrant group in Germany.
3. Schützenfeste = fairs featuring shooting matches; Schützenverein = shooting club.
4. See Glossary.
5. Earl of Galen. The von Galens were an aristocratic Westphalian Catholic family. The most prominent member was Clemens August Earl of Galen (1878–1946), bishop of Münster who preached against the National Socialist euthanasia programme.
6. On 17 October 1939, shortly after the war began, Himmler in the Reich Security Main Office (RSHA) sent the 'Festschreibungserlass' to all police stations, the order preventing freedom of movement of the Sinti and Roma in Germany. This proceeded with the prohibition of self-employment and ghettoisation in communal 'Gypsy internment camps' (Zigeunersammellagern) prior to their deportation. In 1941–2 the social exclusion was extended to include school attendance and children in care, sports clubs, welfare from the National Socialist Peoples' Welfare (Nationalsozialistische Volkswohlfahrt – NSV), the Wehrmacht, and firms producing military supplies followed by the issuing of discriminatory identity cards (Rose, *Den Rauch hatten wir täglich vor Augen*, 1999, Chronology p.363).
7. Romani chib. See Glossary.
8. Börgermoor, Neusustrum and Esterwegen concentration camps comprised Papenburg concentration camp, in Emsland, in 1933.

Endnotes

With the re-organisation of the concentration camp system under the administration of the SS in summer 1934, Börgermoor and Neusustrum were closed and became prisons. Esterwegen continued as a concentration camp until August/September 1936 when its prisoners were transferred to Sachsenhausen and it also became a prison. Initially, political opponents and intellectuals were interned and later other categories of prisoners. The internees were used as forced labour to cultivate the Emsland marshlands and named themselves 'marsh soldiers' (Moorsoldaten) (*Encyclopedia of the Holocaust*, New York, 1990, p.310).

9   Krämermarkt. Krämer = small shopkeeper; markt = Market.
10   See Note 6.
11   The National Socialist Compulsory Labour Service Law (Reichsarbeitsdienstpflichtgesetz) of 26 June 1935 committed young men and women between the ages of 18 and 25 to a compulsory six-month Labour Service. The Reichsarbeitsdienst was a semi-military organisation.
12   On 11 February 1941 the Military High Command ordered the discharge of 'Zigeuner und Zigeunermischlinge' from active military service on 'racial grounds'. Those concerned were to be registered by the police and their names conveyed to the recruiting offices. Those, in the army, navy or air force, were to be transferred to the Supplementary Reserve II or the Territorial Reserve II due to 'lack of suitability' ('wegen mangelnder Eignung') with the observation 'not to be employed' ('n.z.v' = 'nicht zu verwenden'). They were also no longer to receive any military decorations or to be conscripted (O.K.W., 11.2.41, 12 e/f/11 628/40 AHA/Ag/E (1a): Discharge of 'Zigeuner und Zigeunermischlinge' from active military service. In: *Allgemeine Heeresmitteilungen*, 8 (1941), No. 153, pp. 83–4.). The proposed discharge of those concerned presumed that the 'Gypsy characteristics' of the conscripts were known both to their military superiors and to the Military High Command. As, at this point in time, not all Sinti and Roma resident in Germany had been registered, and as the police had only received the directive to collect information regarding 'Gypsies and Gypsy half-castes' enlisted in the armed forces in February 1942, only a few Sinti and Roma were discharged in 1941. Others, like Walter Winter, initially remained in their units. In 1942, the armed forces intensified their policy of exclusion. (Riechert, *Im Gleichschritt ...*, 1994, and Zimmermann, *Rassenutopie und Genozid*, 1996, pp. 193–9).
13   Karl Dönitz (1891–1980). 12 September 1939: Commander of the

German Submarine Fleet. 30 January 1943: Commander of the Navy. On the eve of his suicide Hitler named Dönitz his successor as President of the Reich, Minister of War and Supreme Commander of the Armed Forces. From 2–23 May 1945: Reich 'caretaker government' in Flensburg under Dönitz. The Nuremberg War Crimes Trial sentenced him to ten years' imprisonment for 'crimes against peace'. Released in 1956 (*Encyclopedia of the Holocaust*, New York, 1990, pp. 1490–1).

14 The Reich Security Main Office: On 27 September 1939 Himmler merged the SD and Sipo to become the RSHA. Reinhard Heydrich became its head. It came to comprise seven departments. Department V under Arthur Nebe was the Criminal Police Office (Reichskriminalpolizeiamt), known as the Reich Central Office for Combatting the Gypsy Nuisance, and was specially responsible for the persecution of the Gypsies (*Encyclopedia of the Holocaust*, New York, 1990, pp. 1245–6).

15 Georges Pompidou (1911–74): French politician, Gaullist. 1946–54: member of the Privy Council, 1959–62: member of the Constitutional Council, 1962–8: Prime Minister, 1969–74: President.

16 Auschwitz concentration and death camp comprised three complexes: Auschwitz I Stammlager, Main Camp; Auschwitz II, Auschwitz-Birkenau the death camp where the gas chambers and crematoria operated (Camp section BIIe was the 'Gypsy Camp'); and Auschwitz III, Buna Monowitz, was the industrial camp where prisoners from Auschwitz I and II were employed as slave labour, principally in the chemical concern IG Farben (*Encyclopedia of the Holocaust*, p. 107–19).

17 Walter Winter is registered, as Stanowski Winter, under 'date of arrival in camp', in the Gypsy Camp Register as having entered Birkenau on 14 March 1943 (Memorial Book: *The Gypsies at Auschwitz-Birkenau*, 1993, pp. 912–13).

18 Block. Prisoners' housing. In the Main Camp the blocks were one-story brick buildings. In Birkenau they were brick or wood. (Czech, *Auschwitz Chronicle*, 1990, Glossary, p. 827).

19 The number was preceded by a Z for 'Zigeuner' (Gypsy). In addition to the number tattooed onto the left forearm, prisoners were identified by means of a fabric triangle sewn onto the left shirtfront and right trouser leg. Red signified a political prisoner; green was a criminal prisoner; purple a Jehovah's Witness; black a so-called 'asocial'; pink a homosexual; brown a Zigeuner. Jews wore a six-pointed star. The two triangles forming this would both be

yellow unless the Jewish prisoner also fell into one of the other categories. Eg: a Jewish political prisoner would be identified by a yellow triangle beneath an inverted red triangle (Czech, *Auschwitz Chronicle*, 1990, Glossary, p.829).

20 In the Birkenau 'Gypsy Camp' men and women were numbered separately.

21 Block Senior = Blockältester: An SS-appointed prisoner functionary who was responsible for a block (Czech, *Auschwitz Chronicle*, 1990, Glossary, p.827).

22 Prisoner functionaries were prisoners chosen by the SS to fill certain positions such as Camp Senior, Block Senior, Kapo, etc. (Czech, *Auschwitz Chronicle*, 1990, Glossary, p.829). For information about prisoner functionaries in the Gypsy Camp of Auschwitz-Birkenau, see Smolen, *Das Schicksal*, 1994, pp.150–1, 154; Langbein, *Auschwitz-Prozess*, 1965, vol. 1, p.107 (anonymous witness); H. Braun, in: Spitta/Seybold, *Tag und Nacht*, 1981/2, sheet 167.

23 This refers to the sidings and ramp inside the Birkenau camp. These were completed in May 1944 (Czech, *Auschwitz Chronicle*, 1990, Plans p.3 and p.5; *Auschwitz*, 1982, p.32 and Plan p.38). See p.43.

24 Regarding the short-lived 'canteen' in the Birkenau 'Gypsy Camp' see: APMO Franz Wirbel, 1979, Sheet 10–11; Langbein, *Auschwitz-Prozess*, 1965,Vol. 1, p.143 (Testimony: van Velsen); Langbein, *Menschen in Auschwitz*, 1980, p.167.

25 See Note 22. See also Hierarchy of SS and Prisoner Functionaries in German Concentration Camps, p.141.

26 In most concentration camps there was violent competition between criminal and political prisoners regarding posts as prisoner functionaries which offered the possibility of having some influence over the conditions in the camp.

27 Roll Call Clerk = Blockschreiber. A prisoner functionary who prepared the reports for the SS regarding the camp occupancy level (Czech, *Auschwitz Chronicle*, 1990, Glossary, p.829).

28 The children suffered, in an especially terrible way, from noma, a contagious, gangrenous inflammation of the mouth caused by malnourishment (Adelsberger, *Auschwitz*, 1956, pp.75–6; Müller, Auschwitz Inferno: *The Testimony of a Sonderkommando*, 1979, pp.149–52).

29 A directive from the beginning of April 1943 stipulated that babies and infants were to receive a 'special ration' (Sonderverpflegung) of a half litre of milk or pap with sugar and butter – often misappropriated by the guards and then, after a short period, stopped altogether. The ration for the one- to three-year-olds was

to consist of a litre of milk and a half-litre of soup, and for the three- to six-year-olds a half litre of milk, some butter, white bread, meat soup, jam and chocolate (BAK, NS 19/180, Pohl, WVHA-SS, to Brandt, Personal Staff RF-SS, 9.4.43; RF-SS, Personal Staff, Dr. Brandt, 15.4.43, to Pohl, WVHA.) In reality these 'special rations' were made use of by Dr Joseph Mengele to supplement the food for the children in the 'Kindergarten' in the Gypsy Camp and the around sixty twins who he used for medical experiments before murdering them (Zimmermann, *Rassenutopie*, 1996, pp.349–51).

30 Stubendienst = Block orderly.

31 Roll Call Leader = Rapportführer. A non-commissioned SS officer who was the immediate superior of the camp's Block Commanders or, in Auschwitz-Birkenau, the Block Commanders in one camp section, e.g. BIIe (Gypsy Camp) (Czech, *Auschwitz Chronicle*, 1990, Glossary, p.829).

32 Protective Custody Commander = Schutzhaftlagerführer. An SS officer responsible to the Commandant for the camp or, in Birkenau, a camp section. The title stems from the original euphemism, 'protective custody', for incarceration in a concentration camp (Czech, *Auschwitz Chronicle*, 1990, Glossary, p.829).

33 Ludwig Plagge (1910–48): joined NSDAP on 1 December 1931, and the SS in 1934 where he advanced to SS-Scharführer (Sergeant). Between 20 November 1939 and the end of June 1940 trained in Sachsenhausen for work in concentration camps. From the beginning of July 1940 he was one of the first SS men at Auschwitz. Block Commander in Auschwitz I. Promoted to SS-Oberscharführer (Staff Sergeant) on 1 December 1942. Transferred to Birkenau in 1942. Deputy Roll Call Leader of the Gypsy Camp from its opening through autumn 1943. Acting Protective Custody Commander of the Gypsy Camp in summer 1943. After that worked in Lublin and Flossenbürg. Taken prisoner by US troops on 10 May 1945 and extradited to Poland on 1 March 1947. Sentenced to death on 22 December 1947 and executed on 22 January 1948 (*Memorial Book, The Gypsies at Auschwitz-Birkenau*, 1993, SS-men in the Gypsy Camp, p.1645).

Gerhard Arno Max Palitzsch, (1913–44): NSDAP and SS member. Began as SS-man in concentration camps on 4 August 1933. Promoted to SS-Scharführer (Sergeant) in 1939 during which time he was a guard at the Lichtenberg and Buchenwald concentration camps. Transferred to Sachsenhausen and promoted to SS-

Oberscharführer (Staff Sergeant) on 30 January 1940. On 20 May 1940 he guarded a transport from Sachsenhausen, where he was Block Commander, to Auschwitz where he stayed on as a Roll Call Leader in Auschwitz I until 26 February 1943. Between June and the beginning of October 1943 he was Protective Custody Commander of the Gypsy Camp. At the beginning of October 1943 arrested for theft and transferred to Auschwitz II-Brno (Brünn), and a month later to the SS penal camp at Danzig-Matzkau, and later to the Eastern Front. Unconfirmed killed on 7 December 1944 in Hungary (Memorial Book, *The Gypsies at Auschwitz-Birkenau*, 1993, p. 1644).

Johann Schwarzhuber: Protective Custody Commander in Auschwitz-Birkenau. Rank of SS-Obersturmführer (Lieutenant). Sentenced to death and executed in England in 1947 (Memorial Book, *The Gypsies at Auschwitz-Birkenau*, 1993, p. 1645).

Ernst August König (1919–92): 6 June 1942 transferred from Sachsenhausen concentration camp to Auschwitz. Member of the headquarters staff at Auschwitz II-Birkenau between 30 May and 3 October 1943. Block Commander of the Gypsy Camp. Rank of SS-Unterscharführer (Sergeant). Following investigations carried out by the Central Council of German Sinti and Roma, König was convicted for the multiple murders of concentration camp prisoners by the district court in Siegen. On 24 January 1991, after a forty-three month trial, he was sentenced to life imprisonment. He committed suicide in prison. (*Memorial Book. The Gypsies at Auschwitz-Birkenau*, 1993, p. 1643).

34 Block Commander's room = Blockführerstube. Block Commander's guardhouse (Czech, *Auschwitz Chronicle*, 1990, Glossary, p. 827).

35 Of the total number of 10,849 women and 10,094 men registered in the 'Gypsy Camp' Register, 13,108 (62.6%) came from Germany including the 'Ostmark' of whom there were 2,900 (13.8%) from Austria, 4,380 (20.9%) from Bohemia and Moravia and 1,273 (6.1%) from Poland. The next largest group, comprising 4.8%, were stateless Sinti and Roma, the majority of whom had lived in Germany. Only 3% of other nationalities were registered. 145 were French, 139 Dutch, 121 Belgian; 126 were Yugoslavian, Croatian or Slovakian. Also 34 Hungarians, 27 Russians, 22 Lithuanians, 20 Norwegians and two Spanish were registered. Two people, registered only in the Bunker Book, were Romanian. In addition, there were six Gypsies with Swiss passports, deported from the

Netherlands, but who were not registered as such in Birkenau. The nationality of the remaining 532 (2.54%) in the Register is either indistinct or indecipherable.

Not all deportees were deported from their country of origin. The Norwegians and Spanish were brought to Auschwitz-Birkenau from Belgium, northern France and the Netherlands. The Romanians were deported with the first transport from Germany to Birkenau, on 26 February 1943. The Hungarians had lived either in the 'Old Reich', Posen, or West Prussia, or Vienna, or Burgenland; a Slovakian woman was also deported from here. The Croatians were also not deported from Croatia but from Germany. Prior to their arrest, the 77 deported Yugoslavians principally lived in Kärnten and in Steiermark. (Statistical analysis of the Gypsy Camp Register: *Memorial Book. The Gypsies at Auschwitz-Birkenau*, 1993, pp. 1469–89; regarding prisoner nationality pp. 1469–74. Precise details in Zimmermann, *Rassenutopie*, 1996, pp. 329–30 and pp. 489–90).

36 Corresponding memories from Jewish survivors: Lustig, *Zigeunerlage*, 1985, pp. 16–17; IfZ, Eich 118 Sheet 34, witness Jehuda Bacon.

37 Block Curfew = Blocksperre. Confinement to the blocks (Czech, *Auschwitz Chronicle*, 1990, Glossary, p. 827).

38 Ramp = railway sidings and platform, where the deportees were unloaded and 'selected'. The 'old ramp' was situated near the railway installations between the Main Camp and Birkenau. The 'new ramp', constructed in May 1944, lay within the Birkenau Camp between camp sections BI and BII and led to crematoria 2 and 3 (Czech, *Auschwitz Chronicle*, 1990, Glossary, p. 829). See Note 23 and illustration p. 43.

39 See illustration, p. 92.

40 The IG Farben Buna plant was in Auschwitz III (Monowitz). Buna was the trade name for the synthetic rubber and synthetic fuel produced by I.G. Farben in its Auschwitz plants. I.G. Farben was also the name of the factory, the labour squad that worked there, and the auxiliary camp that belonged to it. The Buna plant was in the village of Monowitz about one and a half kilometres east of the town of Auschwitz. (Czech, *Auschwitz Chronicle*, 1990, Glossary, p. 827).

41 Roll Call Leader (Rapportführer) Hartmann is possibly SS-Sturmmann (Lance Corporal) Kurt Hartmann, who was sentenced to four months imprisonment and expulsion from the SS by the Breslau SS and Police Court for the preferential treatment of prisoners (Langbein, *Menschen in Auschwitz*, 1980, p. 487).

Endnotes

42 Organise = the acquiring, scrounging or pilfering of abandoned goods, SS property or food essential for survival. Appropriation from fellow prisoners, mainly bread, was regarded as theft (Czech, *Auschwitz Chronicle*, 1990, Glossary, p.828).

43 This refers to the area where the subsequent male prisoners' infirmary, section BIIf, was built between the Gypsy Camp BIIe on one side and crematoria 3 and 4 and the 'Canada' personal effects depot on the other. From 23 July 1943, sick Jewish prisoners from the Birkenau camp section BIb were transferred to the male prisoners' infirmary BIIf (Czech, *Auschwitz Chronicle*, 1990, Plan p.5 and p.445). See illustration p.43.

44 Ilse Koch (1906–67). Ilse Köhler married Karl Koch, Commandant of Buchenwald concentration camp, in 1939 and became SS-overseer there. Known as the 'Bitch of Buchenwald' for her sadistic treatment of prisoners. She collected lampshades, book covers, and gloves made from the tattooed skins of specially murdered internees. In 1947 sentenced to life imprisonment in the Buchenwald trial. Released under pardon in 1949 but immediately rearrested and on 15 January 1951 sentenced to life imprisonment. 1967 committed suicide in prison (Wistrich, *Who's Who in Nazi Germany?*, 1995, p.143).

45 Pery Broad (born 23.04.1921): Joined the Hitler Youth in 1931. Joined the SS on 30 January 1942. Trained in the SS-Ersatzbatallion 'Nord'. Transferred to Auschwitz on 23 December 1942 initially as a guard. Later he joined the camp Gestapo. From February 1943 onwards he was Gestapo officer in the Political Department (Department II Camp Gestapo) in the Gypsy Camp where he enforced the sterilisation programme. In January 1945 he was transferred to Buchenwald after the evacuation of Auschwitz. He was taken prisoner by British troops on 6 May 1945 and released in 1947. Arrested again and sentenced to four years imprisonment in the Auschwitz Trial in Frankfurt am Main in 1965. (Charles Schüddekopf, Sketches of some of the Perpetrators. In: Czech, *Auschwitz Chronicle*, 1990, pp.808–9).

The Political Department represented the Reich Security Main Office (RSHA) in the camp. Their function was essentially the keeping of the prisoners' personal files, correspondence with the RSHA and with the Gestapo and Criminal Police there, the reception of prisoner transports, releases, the combating of resistance movements within the camp, the interrogation of prisoners and the administration of the crematoria (*Auschwitz*, 1982, pp.43–4).

46 Block Commander = Blockführer. An SS man responsible for one or more blocks (Czech, *Auschwitz Chronicle*, 1990, Glossary, p.827).

47 See Note 43 concerning the male prisoners' infirmary BIIf.

48 Hermann Diamanski (born 1909), political prisoner, prisoner number 71868. On 30 October 1942 transferred from the Ravensbrück men's camp to Auschwitz. Block Senior and Camp Senior in the Gypsy Camp, thereafter Camp Kapo in Fürstengrube auxiliary camp (Langbein, *Auschwitz-Prozess*, 1965, Vol. 2, p.940). Camp Senior = Lagerälteste. A prisoner functionary appointed by the SS to be a camp representative but answerable to the SS (Czech, *Auschwitz Chronicle*, 1990, Glossary, p.827). Kapo = An SS-appointed foreman of a labour squad. He worked under the SS Squad Leader (Czech, *Auschwitz Chronicle*, 1990, Glossary, p.827).

49 'Selection' = On arrival in Auschwitz the majority of people were directed to one side to die in the gas chambers. The others were designated for forced labour in labour details.

50 'Volksdeutsch' was the Nazi term for ethnic Germans living outside Germany who volunteered or were recruited to join the German forces.

51 Heim in Reich = home to the Reich.

52 Karl Beinski: SS-Rottenführer (Lance Corporal). Block Commander of the Gypsy Camp 1943–4 (*Memorial Book. The Gypsies at Auschwitz-Birkenau*, 1993, p.1640).

53 Romani chib. See Glossary.

54 Sport = punishment drill or exercise.

55 Sinti who collaborated with the police and betrayed members of their own minority group.

56 Jósef Cyrankiewiecz (1911–89). On 4 September 1942 transferred from Montelupich prison, near Krakow, to Auschwitz concentration camp as Resistance Fighter against the occupation of Poland. Prisoner number 62933. One of the leaders of the left-oriented, resistance movement in the Auschwitz camp and the international Auschwitz Combat Group (Czech, *Auschwitz Chronicle*, 1990, p.61, 233, 518–19; Langbein, *Menschen in Auschwitz*, 1980, pp.59–63). 1945 General Secretary of the Polish Socialist Party (PPS) which fused with the Communist Party in 1948. 1947–53 and 1954–70 Prime Minister of Poland, 1970–72 President.

57 Thomas Höllenreiner, born 27 November 1900 in Grotensee. His 'date of arrival in camp' was registered in the Gypsy Camp Register as 9 April 1943, as prisoner number 6052 (*Memorial Book. The Gypsies at Auschwitz-Birkenau*, 1993, pp.1084–5).

58 Dr Josef Mengele (1911–79). At the age of twenty Mengele joined the Stahlhelm (Bund der Frontsoldaten), transferred to the SA in 1934, applied for membership of the NSDAP in 1937 and later for the SS. Studied in Munich, Bonn, Frankfurt am Main and Vienna. 1935 dissertation at the Anthropological Institute of the Philosophy Faculty of Munich University: *Rassenmorphologische Untersuchung des vorderen Unterkieferabschnitts bei vier rassischen Gruppen* (The Racial Morphological Investigation of the Front Submaxilla Section in Four Racial Groups). 1938 medical dissertation: *Sippenuntersuchungen bei Lippen-Kiefer-Gaumensplate* (Genealogical investigation of Lip, Gum and Jaw Fissures). When war began he volunteered for the Waffen-SS. Medical officer in France and the Soviet Union where he was wounded and declared unfit for service. 1943 volunteered for Auschwitz to carry out medical and anthropological experiments. Participated in the 'selection' on the ramp at Auschwitz-Birkenau, lethal injections, shootings and other kinds of deliberate killing of prisoners. Shortly before the evacuation of Auschwitz he returned to Günzburg, Bavaria, his place of birth where, unhindered, he occupied himself with building up the Carl Mengele and Sons agricultural machinery factory. In the mid 1950s he escaped to Latin America where he was able to evade all extradition attempts. Mengele died in 1979 in Brazil due to a swimming accident (Charles Schüddekopf, Sketches of some of the Perpetrators In: Czech, *Auschwitz Chronicle*, 1990, pp.818–19).

59 At the beginning, two blocks, in the Gypsy Camp BIIe, functioned as prisoner infirmary blocks for those imprisoned there; in July 1943 there were five; in autumn 1943 there were six: blocks 22, 24, 26, 28, 30 and 32. The infirmary blocks in camp BIIe were not identical with the male prisoners' infirmary, section BIIf. Regarding topography and division of the Gypsy Camp in Auschwitz-Birkenau see: Memorial Book, 1993 pp.1561–3 and 1572–7; Adelsberger, *Auschwitz*, 1956, pp.44–7; Szymanski, et al, *Krankenbau*, 1987; Smolen, *Das Schicksal*, 1994, pp.146–7.

60 With his projects 'Eye Colour' and 'Specific Proteins', financed by the Kaiser Wilhelm Society and the German Research Council (DFG), Mengele wanted to establish that 'race' and heredity had a fateful influence on human life. The partly heterochromatic eyes of the twins, who Mengele killed by injecting phenol (carbolic acid) into their hearts, were sent to the Kaiser Wilhelm Institute for Anthropology in Berlin-Dahlem for scientific evaluation. Concerning the result of this eye study, Dr Magnussen wrote an

article for the *Zeitschrift für induktiv Abstammungslehre und
Vererbungsforschung* (Journal for Inductive Theory of Evolution and
Genetics), that however did not get published in 1944/5
(Adelsberger, *Auschwitz*, 1956, p.133; Müller-Hill, *Murderous Science*,
1984, pp.71–4; STA Münster, Public Prosecutor Münster 438,
preliminary proceedings against Otmar von Verschuer, in particular
Sheet 55ff, examination of Prof. Dr Hans Nachtsheim, and Sheet
68ff, examination of Dr Karin Magnussen).

61 Sentries = Posten. SS men who guarded the prisoners at work.
Sentry lines. The securing of the camp's borders by means of fences
and sentries. The inner sentry line consisted of concrete piers
connected by electrically charged barbed wire, the whole thing
being illuminated at night. There were watchtowers at 80-metre
intervals. The outer sentry line coincided with the border of the
so-called off-limits zone. The watchtowers were 200 metres apart.
Usually guards were in the watchtowers in the daytime only, until
the labour details returned to the camp. But if a prisoner escaped
the watchtowers of the outer sentry line were occupied for three
days around the clock. The outer perimeter was not secured by any
fencing (Czech, *Auschwitz Chronicle*, 1990, Glossary, pp.829–30).

62 This refers to the men's camp BIId west of the Gypsy Camp BIIe.

63 Rudolf Höß (1900–47). Höß volunteered at the age of fifteen, for
service in the First World War, although under age, and in 1917
was promoted to sergeant on the Turkish Front. 1921 participated
in terrorist actions against the French occupation of the Ruhr and
against the Poles in the struggle for Silesia. Freikorps member. 1922
joined the Nazi Party. 1923 involved, with others, in the murder of
his former teacher who they accused of collaborating with the
French. Sentenced to ten years' imprisonment for participation in
this so-called Parchimer Fememord, but pardoned and released in
1928. 1933 formed an SS cavalry unit. 1934 joined the SS. From
1934 SS guard in Dachau concentration camp, 1935 Block
Commander. 1938 adjutant in Sachsenhausen concentration camp.
1940 Commandant of Auschwitz concentration camp. After the
defeat of Nazi Germany he assumed the name of Franz Lang. 1946
arrested and extradited to Poland. He wrote his autobiography in
Krakow prison in 1946–7: *Commandant in Auschwitz: Autobiography
of Rudolf Höß*. Cleveland 1960. In April 1947 sentenced to death
and hanged in the grounds of the former Auschwitz concentration
camp (Charles Schüddekopf, Sketches of some of the Perpetrators.
In: Czech, *Auschwitz Chronicle*, 1990, p.814).

64 In Birkenau, between 22 March and 25 June 1943, the crematoria 4,

2, 5 and 3 with their accompanying gas chambers were brought into operation, one after the other, to accelerate the process of mass murder (*Auschwitz*, 1982, pp.123–4).

65 The SS, who were responsible for the terrible conditions of the prisoners, used the epidemics that broke out in the Gypsy Camp as grounds to send these prisoners to the gas chambers. So, on 23 March 1943, about 1,700 Gypsies from Bialystok, who had been isolated in blocks 20 and 22 as being suspected of having typhus, were murdered in the gas chambers. A further 1,035 Sinti and Roma who had been deported from Austria, via Bialystok to Birkenau, were also suspected of having typhus by camp doctor Josef Mengele, and were gassed on 25 May 1943 (Czech, *Auschwitz Chronicle*, 1990, pp.358–9, 405).

66 Zyklon B was the trade name for a pesticide. It was a commercial form of hydrogen cyanide which became active on contact with air. It was manufactured by the IG Farben-owned Degesch company and brought to Auschwitz in the summer of 1941 as a vermin-killer and delousing agent.

67 Hermann Langbein also relates this story: Members of a group of Polish Jews transferred from Bergen-Belsen concentration camp to Auschwitz-Birkenau on 23 October 1943, in an act of desperation, put up resistance in the undressing room before the gas chamber. 'The infamous Roll Call Leader Schillinger was so badly wounded that he died on the way to the military hospital in Kattowitz, and SS-Unterscharführer (Corporal) Wilhelm Emmerich so badly wounded that he had a limp after his release from hospital. Rumours have it that a dancer grabbed a revolver from an SS man when he attempted to forcibly undress the hesitant prisoners.' (Langbein, *Menschen in Auschwitz*, 1980, p.143).

Jerzy Tabau's 'The Polish Major's Report', entered as Document L–022 of the Nuremberg International Military Tribunal, identifies the woman as Franceska Mann, a beautiful dancer who was a performer at the Melody Palace nightclub in Warsaw.

68 See Note 56.

69 On 9 November 1943, 100 Sinti and Roma, and towards the end of 1943, an additional 90 Sinti and Roma were transported to Natzweiler concentration camp to be used in medical experiments. From 1944 onward additional Sinti and Roma deemed suitable for work were transferred to concentration camps in Germany. On 15 April 1944, 884 men and 473 women were transported to Buchenwald and Ravensbrück respectively. On 24 May 1944 an additional 144 women were transported to Ravensbrück and 82

men to Flossenbürg (Flossenbürg, end of 1943:Czech, *Auschwitz Chronicle*, 1990, p.522; STA Nuremberg, ND, NO 1059 and 121. Buchenwald and Ravensbrück, April 1944: Czech, *Auschwitz Chronicle*, 1990, p.611; AGKBZH, KL Ravensbrück 65, Transport Lists 21–30 April 1944, special transport–transfer from Auschwitz, 19 April 1944. Ravensbrück, May 1944: Czech, *Auschwitz Chronicle*, 1990, p.632; AGKBZH, KL Ravensbrück 66, transfer from Auschwitz 27 May 1944.). These transports returned to Germany because, from the end of the year 1943–4 onward, due to the precarious situation at the front for Nazi Germany, increasing numbers of concentration camp prisoners had to replace the insufficient number of POWs and civilian workers within German industry.

70 Orderly room = Schreibstube. These offices regulated and recorded all the internal activities of the camp: admissions, assignment to residential blocks, maintaining files and card indexes, etc. They were run entirely by prisoners (Czech, *Auschwitz Chronicle*, 1990, Glossary, p.828).

71 See, p.77–8.

72 Sometimes this day is dated as the end of July 1944. On this day, the former Wehrmacht soldiers in the Gypsy Camp, with their family members and others, were assessed to be fit for work by the SS, loaded onto lorries and taken to blocks 10 and 11 of Auschwitz Main Camp (Czech, *Auschwitz Chronicle*, 1990, p.677).

73 In mid May 1944, the orderly room was instructed to register all German and Austrian Sinti and Roma, and their families, who, prior to their arrest, had served in the German armed services, possessed a military decoration, or who still had relatives in the armed forces. Those former Wehrmacht soldiers who were prepared to be sterilised were promised their liberty. They were transferred to blocks 10 and 11 of Auschwitz Main Camp. The planned sterilisation did not take place. At the end of the year 1944–5 camp doctor Dr Franz Lucas attempted to carry out this procedure in Ravensbrück concentration camp. Many were able to avoid this (Czech, *Auschwitz Chronicle*, 1990, p.628 and 631; Langbein, *Auschwitz-Prozess*, 1965, Vol. 1, p.107 [anonymous witness], p.108 [testimony Stein], p.523 [testimony Steinberg], Vol. 2, p.613 [testimony Stein], p.615 [testimony Lucas]).

Erich Winter relates: 'I was to be released on condition that I be sterilised. I didn't want to do this but my brother and sister said: 'Do it. Do it. When you're out, you'll have more chance of helping us than you have in here. Here you can't do anything.' Well, I let

myself be persuaded and was taken to block 11 in Auschwitz Main
Camp.'

74 The SS staged this farewell ceremony, exceptional in the Auschwitz
camp history, with the intention of deluding both groups into a
sense of security. Those remaining in Auschwitz were led to believe
that the transport was an advance squad leaving for a better,
purposely conceived camp for Gypsies in which they would soon
meet them again (Zimmermann, *Rassenutopie*, 1996, pp.342–3).

75 On 2 August 1944 the SS imposed a camp curfew on the entire
Birkenau camp. Armed SS surrounded the Gypsy Camp. A total of
2,897 people, some of whom offered resistance to the end, were
taken by lorry, in half-hour intervals, to crematoria 2 and 5 and
murdered in the gas chambers (Zimmermann, *Rassenutopie*, 1996,
pp.342–3).

76 There were 490 women and children under twelve years old and
213 men – 199 of German nationality and 14 stateless – brought to
Ravensbrück from Auschwitz-Birkenau at the end of
July/beginning of August. In Ravensbrück the men were given the
prisoner numbers 9509 to 9719 as well as 9722 and 9723. These
male Gypsy prisoners were mainly former Wehrmacht soldiers,
whom the SS had promised liberty under the condition of
sterilisation and who had been transferred to blocks 10 and 11 in
Auschwitz I Main Camp during the last half of May 1944, as well
as additional former Wehrmacht soldiers (AGKBZH, KL
Ravensbrück 50, Sheets 47–50, Delivery of Gypsies, undated;
Czech, *Auschwitz Chronicle*, 1990, p.677; Langbein, *Auschwitz-
Prozess*, 1965, Vol. 1, p.107 [anonymous witness]; Vol. 1, p.108, and
Vol. 2, p.613 [testimony Stein], p.615 [testimony Lucas], p.617
[anonymous witness]).

77 Walter Winter and his brother Erich were registered with the
prisoner numbers 9573 and 9574 respectively (AGKBZH, KL
Ravensbrück 50, Sheet 49).

78 The men's camp of Ravensbrück concentration camp was
constructed adjacent to the women's camp in March/April 1941.
Initially, there were 350 male prisoners transferred here from
Sachsenhausen. Administratively, the men's camp belonged to the
Main Camp; the camp Commandant was subordinate to the
Commandant of the Main Camp. In 1943–4 there was an average
of 1,500 to 2,000 male prisoners imprisoned in five blocks. In
August 1943 this number rose to 3,100. From mid 1943 eight
auxiliary camps: Barth, Dabelow, Kaliies, Karlshagen I and II,
Klützow, Neubrandenburg, Rechlin and Stargard, were established

which, at times, brought the numbers of prisoners up to 6,000. The sickness rate was extremely high in the Ravensbrück men's camp.

Between 1941 and 1943, 20,086 male prisoners were registered in Ravensbrück; 7,513 were transferred from here to other concentration camps. Around 16 per cent were Jews of various nationalities. Political prisoners were in the majority, being around 80 percent. Regarding nationality, Poles, with over 6,400, were in the majority, then came Germans (almost 4,000), then Russians (around 3,850) and French (around 2,250). 1,617 prisoners died in Ravensbrück and 317 were released (Arnt, Ravensbrück, 1970, pp. 116–17).

79 Wittenberge concentration camp was a satellite camp of Neuengamme concentration camp. It was established on the grounds of the former Pulp and Rayon Staple Factory Wittenberge. Prisoners worked as forced labour in this factory.

80 Stubbenkommando = work detail that had to clear woodland.

81 The lad probably belonged to those Roma deported to Auschwitz from the Austrian Burgenland, on the border with Hungary. The majority of Burgenland Roma had Hungarian names.

82 Dog squadron = Hundestaffel. An SS kennel of Alsatians and bloodhounds specially trained to guard people wearing striped uniform. These were principally employed guarding labour details working outside the outer sentry line (Czech, *Auschwitz Chronicle*, 1990, Glossary, p. 828).

83 The traditional culture of the Sinti forbids the consumption of horsemeat (see also Note 1).

84 See Note 57.

85 See Note 73.

86 See Note 57.

87 Of those Sinti and Roma transferred from Auschwitz-Birkenau to Ravensbrück two escaped, seven were released, and on 30 September 1944 eight were transferred to Bergen-Belsen concentration camp. On 3 March 1945 the rest were transferred to Sachsenhausen concentration camp. (AGKBZH; KL Ravensbrück 50, Sheets 47–50, Delivery of Gypsies).

88 Initially, Erich and Walter Winter were assigned to Block 58 in the small camp of Sachsenhausen concentration camp, where new prisoners were isolated. A little to the rear, in a separate area, was the 'cell block' (Zellenbau), the Gestapo camp prison. Walter Winter was later transferred to a block in the large camp, whereas Erich Winter had to remain in the small camp. Regarding the topography and history of Sachsenhausen concentration camp, see

Kühn, *Konzentrationslager Sachsenhausen*, 1990.

89 Anton Kaindl was the last Commandant of Sachsenhausen concentration camp. He was handed over by the British to the Soviet war crimes authorities for trial in July 1946. He was tried by a Soviet court on 1 November 1947 and sentenced to life imprisonment.

90 SS-Oberführer Dr Oskar Dirlewanger (1895–1945) formed his brigade in 1940 from former concentration camp inmates convicted of poaching, replacing casualties with Soviet deserters and criminals. Sonderkommando Dirlewanger operated behind the front lines during the German invasion of the Soviet Union. The unit was infamous for barbarous 'counter-insurgency' operations i.e. raping, looting and killing. The division was reportedly surrounded by the Soviets and massacred during the final battles in Berlin during late April 1945. Dirlewanger was wounded and ended up in Soviet captivity but was sent back to Germany. He was recovering from his wounds in a hospital in Althausen, Bavaria, when on 1 June 1945 French occupation forces used Polish soldiers to bring him to Althausen prison. He was beaten and tortured by his Polish guards and died during the night of 4/5 June (Auerbach, *Einheit Dirlewanger*, 1912; Klausch, *Antifaschisten in SS-Uniform*, 1993; Maclean, *The Cruel Hunters*, 1998).

91 Local Chapter Leader = Ortsgruppenleiter. An NSDAP functionary below the district level. In the country an NSDAP Ortsgruppe included one or more village community; in the towns it corresponded to a ward.

92 See Note 3. Hof = yard.

93 Apart from English, all the Indo-European languages, including German, have both a formal 'you' – 'Sie' and a familiar 'you' – 'du'. It is not merely a matter of grammar but of culture too. German-speakers tend to keep their distance longer with acquaintances and it can become very uncomfortable when the du/Sie rules are broken.

94 Denazification was the attempt to eliminate Nazi ideology and Nazi functionaries from public life. However, against the background of reconstruction and the Cold War, the legal and political investigation of individual guilt soon became of secondary importance. On 12 October 1946 a regulation issued by the Allied Control Council for Germany required that former Nazis be classified as: 1. major offenders; 2. offenders. 3. lesser offenders; 4. followers or 5. persons exonerated. Persons in categories 1 to 4 were subject to some sort of punishment, although those born after

1919 in category 4 received a 'youth amnesty'. The basis for classification was a questionnaire. It was not rare for nominal Nazis to receive severe punishment whereas ardent Nazis went unpunished. Because of the difficulty of implementation, in 1947 and 1948 it was decided to turn the denazification process over to the German authorities (*Encyclopedia of the Holocaust*, New York, 1990, pp. 359–62).

95 Prior to the currency reform in 1948, food and other necessities were rationed and obtainable only through officially allocated coupons.

96 The currency reform was announced on 20 June 1948. The new currency, the Deutschmark, was printed in the US and made its way to Germany in huge boxes with the deliberately misleading label 'Bird Dog', closely guarded by army soldiers. On the first day, everybody was allowed to exchange 40 Reichsmark for Deutschmark at the rate of 1:1. The Euro replaced the Deutschmark on 1 January 2002 (*Death of the Deutschmark*, BBC, 2001).

97 There were a number of SS Panzer Divisions such as the 1st SS Panzer Division 'Leibstandarte Adolf Hitler', the 2nd SS Panzer Division 'Das Reich' and the 3rd SS Panzer Division 'Totenkopf'.

The Hierarchy of SS and Prisoner Functionaries in German Concentration Camps

Concentration camps were administered by the Reich Security Main Office (RSHA) in Berlin.

SS Personnel	Prisoner Functionaries
Administration:	
Camp Commandant (Lagerführer)	
Protective Custody Commander (Schutzhaftlagerführer)	
Roll Call Leader (Rapportführer)	Camp Senior (Lagerältester)
Block Commander (Blockführer)	Block Senior (Blockältester)
	Camp Clerk (Lagerschreiber)
	Roll Call Clerk (Blockschreiber)
	Block Orderly (Stubendienst)
Forced Labour Department:	
Labour Commandant (Arbeitseinsatzführer)	Forced Labour Official (Arbeitseinsatz)
Labour Detail Leader (Kommandoführer)	Kapo (Head of a Labour Detail)
Medical Department:	
Camp Doctor (Lagerarzt)	Head Prisoner Doctor (Erster Häftlingsarzt)
SS Doctors	Infirmary Clerk (Revierschreiber)
	Block Doctor (Blockarzt)
Political Department:	
Gestapo Officer	

The political department received its orders directly from Gestapo headquarters.

Chronology of the National Socialist Persecution of the Sinti and Roma

Pre-1933

The persecution of the German Sinti and Roma did not begin with National Socialism. Prior to this period they had suffered centuries of discrimination and persecution legitimated through edicts and Gypsy laws.

In 1899, within the framework of making what was considered to be the legitimate battle against Gypsies more efficient, a Gypsy Information Agency under the direction of Alfred Dillmann was established in the police headquarters in Munich, Bavaria. A register of all Gypsies over the age of six began to be compiled including genealogical data, photographs and fingerprints, property and movement, and in particular information relating to 'criminality'. In 1905 Dillmann published the results in his 'Zigeuner-Buch'. He re-emphasised the racist idea of the Gypsies' genetic tendency toward criminal behaviour and stressed the dangers of a mixed 'Gypsy' and German gene pool. In 1909 a central registry of fingerprints was opened. In December 1911 a conference was organised at which the Munich Register was used as a basis for a larger database by incorporating data from the registers of six other German states. In 1913 additional information regarding indictments from the public prosecutor and births, deaths and marriages from population registration offices was collected. When, in 1938, Himmler took possession of these files 30,000 individuals had been registered.

In 1920 Karl Binding and Alfred Hoche published their

book, *Die Freigabe der Vernichtung lebensunwerten Lebens* (The Eradication of Lives Undeserving of Life) in which they argued for the killing of those who were 'Ballastexistenzen', i.e. those whose lives were seen merely as ballast, or dead weight, within humanity. Perceived Gypsy 'criminality' was seen as a transmitted genetic disease. The concept of 'lives undeserving of life' became central to Nazi race policy when on 14 July 1933 the Law to Prevent Hereditary Diseases was passed. Euthanasia and sterilisation were deemed legitimate methods of control.

Even though 'Gypsies' enjoyed full and equal rights of citizenship under Article 109 of the Weimar Constitution, they were subject to special, discriminatory laws. A Bavarian law of 16 July 1926 outlined measures for "Combating Gypsies, Vagabonds, and the Workshy" and required the systematic registration of all Sinti and Roma. The law prohibited Gypsies from "roaming about or camping in bands", and those "Gypsies unable to prove regular employment" risked being sentenced to forced labour for up to two years. This law became the national norm in 1929.

In November 1927, the Prussian Ministry of the Interior required all "Gypsies and non-Gypsy vagrants" to constantly carry identity cards containing a photo and fingerprints.

A so-called German Society for Racial Hygiene was founded by Alfred Ploetz as early as 1905. Three German professors, E. Baur, E. Fischer and F. Lenz, published *Menschliche Erblichkeitslehre und Rassenhygiene* (Human Heredity and Racial Hygiene) in two volumes in Munich 1927 and 1931 respectively which formed the basis of Nazi racial hubris. They concluded: "To prevent the reproduction of asocial or otherwise seriously degenerate individuals, legislation should be immediately introduced to secure their segregation in labour colonies."

In 1929 the 1899 Munich Gypsy Information Agency became the Central Office for Combating the Gypsy Nuisance and in 1933, just ten days before the Nazis came to power, local government officials in Burgenland, Austria, called for the withdrawal of all civil rights from 'Gypsies'.

In Germany between 1900 and 1933 there were a total of 150 decrees enacted against Sinti and Roma. Terminology such as "combating the Gypsy plague" and "bands" or "hordes" was used. This was the fertile soil upon which Nazi racism was built.

1933
The first imprisonments of Sinti and Roma followed by prohibition from pursuing their professions, and numerous other measures that exclude them from all spheres of public life.

15 September 1935
Promulgation of the Nuremberg Race Laws (Nürnberger Rassengesetze). Reich Minister of the Interior, Wilhelm Frick, says on 3 January 1936: "Jews and Gypsies are the only races of foreign blood in Europe." Intermarriage between Sinti and non-Sinti is forbidden.

Spring 1936
The establishment of the Research Centre for Racial Hygiene and Population Biology (Rassenhygienische Forschungsstelle (RHF) in Berlin under the direction of Dr Robert Ritter. Ritter and his team begin to carry out 'racial hygiene' (rassenbiologische) evaluations throughout Reich territory.

July 1936
In the run-up to the Berlin Olympic Games hundreds of Berlin Sinti and Roma are interned in the Berlin-Marzahn camp. Other such communal internment camps are established in other cities.

June 1938
Hundreds of Sinti and Roma are interned in the concentra-

tion camps Sachsenhausen, Dachau, Buchenwald and later Mauthausen and other concentration camps.

1 October 1938
Absorption of the National Socialist Gypsy Police Department (Zigeunerpolizeistelle) in Munich by the Reich Criminal Police Department (Reichskriminalpolizeiamt) in Berlin (from 27 September 1939 Department V of the Reich Security Main Office [RSHA]) under the leadership of SS-Oberführer Arthur Nebe. In close co-operation with the Racial Hygiene Research Unit (Rassenhygienische Forschungsstelle) data about Sinti and Roma is systematically collected as a basis for further persecution.

8 December 1938
Himmler's Basic Decree (Grunderlass) declares "the Gypsy Question must be resolved on the grounds of race". Himmler orders the registration and 'racial hygiene' (rassenbiologische) evaluations of all Sinti and Roma in Germany. This task is assigned to the Racial Hygiene Research Centre (Rassenhygienische Forschungsstelle).

21 September 1939
Conference of department heads of the Security Police and leaders of the SS Einsatzgruppen (special action groups), under the chairmanship of Reinhard Heydrich. It is decided to deport all Sinti and Roma and Jews from the Reich territory to occupied Poland.

13 October 1939
SS-Hauptsturmführer Walter Braune informs Eichmann of SS-Oberführer Nebe's request for "information as to when he can send the Berlin Gypsies."

16 October 1939
The SD-Donau informs SS-Oberführer Nebe that the first

transport of Jews departing Vienna on 20 October 1939 "could be coupled with three or four wagons of Gypsies."

17 October 1939
Himmler's Enabling Order (Festschreibungserlass). All Sinti and Roma are forbidden to leave their place of residence under threat of internment in concentration camps.

30 January 1940
Heydrich holds a conference with SS leaders confirming the intention to deport "all Jews in the new Ostgaue and 30,000 Gypsies from the Reich territory to the General Government in Poland."

27 April 1940
Himmler's order concerning the deportation of 2,500 German Sinti and Roma to occupied Poland. The deportation trains with Sinti and Roma families began departing in May from Hamburg, Cologne and Hohenasperg near Stuttgart to the 'General Government' in Poland.

7 August 1941
An order from Himmler states that the Reich Criminal Police Department (Department V of the RSHA) is to decide on further deportations of Sinti and Roma to concentration camps on the grounds of 'race reports' (Rassegutachten). The Racial Hygiene Research Unit produces around 24,000 such 'reports' by the end of 1944.

From summer 1941
Sinti and Roma are systematically shot behind the eastern front by SS Einsatzgruppen, units of the Wehrmacht and the Order Police (Ordnungspolizei). SS Einsatzgruppen leader Otto Ohlendorf states in the Nuremberg war crimes trial: "There was no distinction made between Gypsies and Jews, the same order applied to both."

10 October 1941
Conference in Prague under the direction of Reinhard Heydrich "concerning the solution of the Jewish Question" and "the evacuation of the Gypsies in the Protectorate of Bohemia and Moravia."

November 1941
The deportation of around 5,000 Sinti and Roma from Burgenland, Austria, to Lodz where a Gypsy ghetto is established inside the Jewish ghetto. Hundreds die there from diseases and epidemics. In January 1942 the survivors are deported to Chelmno death camp and asphyxiated by the exhaust fumes of gas vans.

February 1942
East Prussian Sinti and Roma, mostly farmers, are deported to Bialystok concentration camp and later from there via Brest-Litowsk to Auschwitz.

7 July 1942
The Reichskommissar for Ostland concerning the 'Gypsies': "I order that they be treated the same as the Jews."

29 August 1942
Harald Turner, chief of the German Administration in Serbia, announces that Serbia is the only country in which the "Jewish question and the Gypsy question" have been solved.

14 September 1942
Reich Minister of Justice Otto Thierack minutes a meeting with Joseph Goebbels: "With regard to the extermination of 'asocial' life, Dr Goebbels is of the opinion that Jews and Gypsies are quite simply to be exterminated. The idea of extermination through work is the best."

3 December 1942
Secret letter from the head of the Party Chancellery, Martin Bormann, from the "Führer's headquarters" to Heinrich Himmler in the RSHA, stating that: "The Führer would not approve of individual 'Gypsies' being excluded from the 'current measures' of extermination for reasons of 'research into German customs'."

16 December 1942
Himmler's Auschwitz Decree is the trigger for the deportation of 23,000 Sinti and Roma from German-occupied Europe, including 13,000 from the Reich territory that begins at the end of February 1943, to the section of Auschwitz-Birkenau death camp termed the "Gypsy Camp".

May 1943
Dr Josef Mengele becomes SS camp doctor in Auschwitz. His first action is to 'select' several hundred Sinti and Roma to be gassed. He continues his 'research into twins', supported by the German Research Foundation (Deutsche Forschungsgemeinschaft) and the Kaiser Wilhelm Institute, through the killing of Jewish, and Sinti and Roma children.

16 May 1944
The attempt by Auschwitz Commandant Rudolf Höß to send the remaining 6,000 Sinti and Roma in the "Gypsy Camp" to the gas chambers collapses in the face of the resistance from the men armed with spades, poles and stones.

2 August 1944
Dissolution of the "Gypsy Camp" in Auschwitz-Birkenau. The remaining, around 2,900 survivors of this "Gypsy Camp" section, mostly women, children and elderly people, are murdered in the gas chambers on the night of 3 August. Prior to this around 3,000 Sinti and Roma are deported to other con-

centration camps in the Reich territory as slave labour for the armament industry.

May 1945
The number of Sinti and Roma murdered in concentration camps by the Wehrmacht and SS Einsatzgruppen by the end of the war is estimated at half a million. Of the 40,000 German and Austrian Sinti and Roma registered by the Nazis, more than 25,000 were murdered.

Origin and History of the Roma
and Sinti

Today at least four major groups of 'Gypsies' are recognised: the *Banjara* in India, the *Dom* in the Middle East, the *Lom* in Turkey and the Caucasus, and the *Rom* or *Roma* in Europe, who have also migrated to other parts of the world.

Linguistic research indicates that these peoples originated from the Punjab region of north-west India. It is thought they left their homeland in separate groups at different periods between 700 and 1000AD due to Arabian invasions and conquest of Persia and north India. Their westward migration took them to Persia, Armenia, Byzantium and Greece. The Roma language contains loan-words from Persian, Armenian and Greek. Between the eleventh and fourteenth centuries they settled in the Balkans, the Middle East and Eastern Europe. In Moravia and Walachia they were enslaved from 1400 to 1856.

This westward migration reached central Europe in the fifteenth century, for example, Böhmen 1399, Hildesheim 1407, Hessen and Basel 1414, Meissen 1416, Zürich, Magdeburg and Lübeck 1417, Elsace and Sachsen 1418. They had reached Spain, Sweden and England by the sixteenth century. Their appearance, language, customs and itinerant way of life set them apart from the settled population and led to numerous prejudices causing their terrible persecution throughout the entire early modern period. They were accused of being beggars, thieves and spies, and regarded as heathens or allies of the Devil. They became scapegoats for all manner of evils.

Roma were occupied in petty trade, handicrafts and music. They generally adopted the religion of the lands in which they settled, for example, Islam in Bosnia and the Crimea, Orthodoxy in Serbia, and Roman Catholicism in Europe. They were oppressed, persecuted and ultimately banished from many provinces, such as Lucerne in 1471, Brandenburg in 1482 and Spain in 1484. In 1496/7 the Imperial Diet of the Holy Roman Empire outlawed them and sanctioned their persecution, torture and murder. At the beginning of the sixteenth century Portugal, France, England, Scotland, Flanders, Holland, Denmark, Bohemia, Poland and Lithuania introduced similar legislation. In 1561 the parliament of Orléans resolved to exterminate them by fire and sword.

The harshest legislation was enacted within the Holy Roman Empire. Between 1497 and 1774 a total of 146 edicts were enacted permitting all kinds of physical and mental violence and banishment from German lands. In 1726 Emperor Charles VI, father of Maria Theresia, decreed that all male Sinti and Roma be put to death and all Sinti and Roma women and children have one ear cut off.

Empress Maria Theresia and her son, Emperor Joseph II, sought to forcibly assimilate the Gypsies and make them take up sedentary lives through compulsory military service, prohibition of horse ownership, compulsory mixed marriage, prohibition of their language and traditional dress, compulsion to learn a trade, removal of their own jurisdiction and registration. Sinti and Roma children were removed from their families from the age of four to be brought up as Christians. In 1775 Frederick the Great of Prussia established a 'Gypsy village' in Friedrichslohra (today Großlohra).

When in 1856 slavery was abolished in Moldavia and Walachia, around 200,000 liberated Roma migrated westwards. The differences in their history of repression, traditions and dialects from those of the west European Sinti resulted in the two groups remaining autonomous of one another. Until the end of the nineteenth century both groups were equally affected by increasingly repressive measures and subject to special registration and surveillance procedures.

In contrast, in the nineteenth and at the beginning of the twentieth century an illusory image of the south-east European Roma became the source of a romantic interest in the European 'noble savage'. This romantic image of the 'Gypsy' was depicted in practically every art form, e.g., the music of Franz Liszt (1811–86) and his book *The Gypsy in Music* (1860); Romantic composers Johannes Brahms, Anton Dvorak, Franz Liszt, Robert Schumann and Peter Tchaikovsky transcribed *lieder* with such titles as *Gypsy Songs* and *Gypsy Melodies*; in opera and operetta such as Giuseppe Verdi's *Il Travatore* (1853), Bizet's *Carmen* (1875), Johann Strauss' *The Gypsy Baron* (1885) and Franz Lehar's *Gypsy Love* (1910); in chamber and orchestral music such as Maurice Ravel's *Tzigane* (1822–24) in Leni Riefenstahl's film *Tiefland* (1953); in the novels and poetry of Hermann Hesse; the paintings of Otto Müller (e.g. *Die Zigeuner Mappe* – a series of lithographs); and D.H. Lawrence's *The Virgin and the Gypsy*. Even today restaurant menus offer *Zigeunerschnitzel* (pork escalope served in spicy sauce with red and green peppers), *Zigeunersteak* and *Zigeunerblut* (Gypsy blood, a type of cheap red wine).

In Germany at the end of the nineteenth century the name 'Zigeuner' increasingly assumed a biologically determined racist meaning. Contrary to Article 104 of the Weimar constitution, guaranteeing all Germans equality before the law, police harassment increased dramatically. In 1899 a Gypsy Information Agency was set up in Munich with a special register. In 1906 a directive on "Combating the Gypsy Nuisance" (Bekämpfung des Zigeunerunwesens) was enacted in Prussia with bilateral agreements with Austria-Hungary, Italy, Switzerland, France, Belgium, the Netherlands, Luxembourg and Russia. In 1926 a "law to combat Gypsies, vagrants, and 'workshys'" was enacted in Bavaria. In 1929 the Munich Gypsy Agency became the Central Office for Combating the Gypsy Nuisance (see also page 142).

Postscript: Sinti and Roma in post-war Germany

━━━

The Continuity of Anti-Gypsyism after 1945
The Romani word for the Nazi genocide is *Porrajmos*, (paw-RYE-mos) which means 'the Devouring'.
The defeat of the Nazi regime ended the ideology of racial cleansing. However, the liberated German Sinti and Roma survivors of the concentration camps and Porrajmos returned home to be again confronted with repression and discrimination by the police, housing, health and welfare authorities.
Most were denied victim status. Only those groups persecuted on grounds of political opposition, race, belief or ideology were eligible for compensation. It was argued that 'Gypsies' were not persecuted for racial motives but because of their asocial and criminal behaviour. For this reason they were not officially regarded as 'victims of Nazism' and consequently not eligible for compensation. On the contrary, they became subject to criminal investigation once again. Moreover, the same 'Gypsy specialists' remained in the Criminal Police after the war and continued the so-called "campaign against the Gypsy nuisance" which, during the Nazi period, had been responsible for the recording, registering and collection of data on all "Gypsies and vagrants" in the Third Reich and which led to their persecution, deportation and subsequent genocide. These officials also often appeared as 'experts' in compensation proceedings allowing the perpetrators to determine the validity of survivors' claims. In the immediate

post-war period denial of claims was the rule. The authorities also questioned their German citizenship and some were declared stateless.

Although in 1947 the Western Allies revoked the legislation of the Weimar Republic and the Third Reich, the federal states passed 'vagrant regulations', i.e. special laws regulating Sinti and Roma which essentially corresponded with the racist laws and decrees of the Nazi period (in contravention of Article 3 of the Basic Constitutional Law of 23 May 1949). The Vagrant Centre (Landfahrerzentrale) of the Bavarian police continued to use the "index cards and files of Gypsies" from the former Reich Centre for Combating the Gypsy Nuisance (Reichzentrale zur Bekämpfung des Zigeunerunwesens) and made these the basis of their police policy. Only in the 1970s, after the Sinti and Roma activists demanded access to these index cards and files was it alleged that they had been destroyed. However, police harassment and discrimination against Sinti and Roma continued into the middle of the 1980s. On the basis of these Nazi files the Vagrant Centre not only further pursued the registration of the entire Sinti and Roma population but also police training continued to be racist and to be given by 'Gypsy experts' from the former Reich Security Main Office (RSHA).

The post-war denazification programme was inconsequent and incomplete. Prominent individuals in the Criminal Police and academics in the Research Centre for Racial Hygiene and Population Biology (Rassenhygienische Forschungsstelle) responsible for the genocide of the Sinti and Roma were not only never brought to justice, but successfully pursued their careers after the war.

The crimes committed against the Sinti and Roma generally played a very subordinate role in the major trials against concentration camp personnel, Einsatzgruppen and members of the police who, among others, were involved in the systematic killing of Gypsies in Eastern Europe.

As head of the Criminal Police, Arthur Nebe's role in the

deportation of the Sinti and Roma to concentration camps has been overshadowed by his complicity, and subsequent execution, in the Stauffenberg assassination attempt on Hitler on 20 July 1944. Paul Werner, Nebe's deputy and responsible for the May deportations to Poland, pursued a career as a civil servant after the war. Joseph Eichberger (RSHA), directly responsible for organising the deportation of the Sinti and Roma to concentration camps (comparable to Adolf Eichmann in the case of the Jews), became head of the 'Gypsy' department (Nachrichtenstelle über Zigeuner) of the Bavarian police. Leo Karsten, head of the Office for Gypsy Affairs (Dienststelle für Zigeunerfragen) in the RKPA, became head of the Migrant Department (Landfahrerstelle) of the Baden police. Hans Maly, a senior officer in Department V A2, the department for preventive measures against asocials, prostitutes and 'Gypsies', became head of the Bonn criminal police.[1] Only in 1990, following investigations carried out by the Central Council of German Sinti and Roma, was SS-Unterscharführer Ernst August König, Block Commander of the Gypsy Camp of Auschwitz-Birkenau, convicted for the multiple murders of concentration camp prisoners by the district court in Siegen. On 24 January 1991, after a forty-three month trial, he was sentenced to life imprisonment.[2]

The 'race scientists' and 'Gypsy experts' were also not brought to trial and successfully continued their careers after the war. The criminal investigations initiated into the former head of the Research Centre for Racial Hygiene, Robert Ritter and his assistant Eva Justin, on account of their complicity in the forced sterilisation and deportation of Sinti and Roma to Auschwitz-Birkenau, were discontinued in their

1   Daniel Strauß, "da muss man wahrhaft alle Humanität ausschalten..." Zur Nachkriegsgeschichte der Sinti und Roma in Deutschland. In: Landeszentrale für politische Bildung Baden-Württemberg;Verband Deutscher Sinti und Roma Landesverband Baden-Württemberg (ed.): "Zwischen Romantisierung und Rassismus". *Sinti und Roma 600 Jahre in Deutschland*. Stuttgart 1998, pp. 26–36.

2   Romani Rose, Bergerrechte für Sinti und Roma. *Das Buch zum Rassismus in Deutschland*. Heidelberg 1987.

preliminary stages and they were not brought to trial. The former 'racial hygiene researcher', Hermann Arnold, inherited the 'race reports' (Rassegutachten), genealogical trees, card indexes, photographs and films. As medical officer of the Landau public health department he was an "expert for Gypsy questions" with the Federal Ministry for Youth and Family Affairs and was additionally employed as advisor for the "spiritual welfare of Gypsies" with the Catholic Bishops' Conference until 1979. Himmler's documents for the planning of the genocide of the Sinti and Roma were at the disposal of the 'Gypsy specialists' with the police from Munich to Hamburg and continued to serve for the control and surveillance of this national minority. In 1947, Sophie Ehrhardt, another former employee of the Research Centre for Racial Hygiene, against whom the Cologne Director of Prosecutions started a judicial inquiry in 1961 and discontinued in 1963, took over the so-called "anthropological index" in her institute at the University of Tübingen. This index contained a collection of photographs, hand prints, skull measurements with separate measurements of nostrils, eyes, etc. In 1949 she qualified as a university lecturer and in 1958 she became professor in Tübingen. As late as 1969 and 1974 respectively she published articles about the "Gypsy skull" and the "lines of the hands of Gypsies". Dr Adolf Würth, another 'racial hygiene researcher' became an official in the Bureau of Statistics in Baden-Württemberg. A judicial inquiry into his work was also discontinued.[3]

Following protests by Sinti and Roma, the files of the genocide programme, which Hermann Arnold and Sophie Ehrhardt made use of for decades after 1945, were transferred to the Federal Archive in Koblenz. Today the files of around 20,000 murdered Sinti and Roma are deposited there but the 'race

---

3   Sybil Milton, Persecuting the Survivors: The Continuity of 'Anti-Gypsyism' in Postwar Germany and Austria. In: Susan Tebbutt (ed.), Sinti and Roma. Gypsies in German-Speaking Society and Literature. New York and Oxford 1998.

reports', i.e. the actual death sentences, were allegedly mislaid between Landau and Tübingen.

Josef Mengele, the Auschwitz camp doctor who carried out pseudo-scientific experiments on Sinti and Roma twins, was helped to escape to South America where he successfully evaded extradition. Professor Otmar Freiherr von Verschuer, head of the Kaiser Wilhelm Institute for Anthropology, Human Genetics and Eugenics in Berlin, subsidised and collaborated in Mengele's experiments and acquired "examined material" from him such as the eyes of murdered 'Gypsy' twins and serum from twins he had infected with typhus. Verschuer was neither investigated nor indicted. In 1951 he was appointed Professor and Director of the Institute of Human Genetics at the Medical School of the University of Münster.

Research carried out during the Nazi period was published post-war in academic publications. For example, Heinrich Hufmann's dissertation *Äußere Beckenmaße und geschlechtliche Entwicklung bei Zigeunerinnen* (Exterior Pelvic Measurements and the Sexual Development of Female Gypsies) published in 1952 made involuntary use of Roma women who had survived the Wehrmacht massacre of 200 male Roma in Serbia. Johann Knobloch's 1953 publication *Romani-Texte aus dem Burgenland* (Romani Texts from Burgenland) was researched at the Lackenbach 'Gypsy internment camp' before the Roma were deported to Auschwitz.[4] Hermann Arnold's various post-war 'Zigeuner' publications continued to reflect his racist thinking. Leni Riefenstahl's film *Tiefland*, first shown in 1954, made use of Sinti and Roma from the Berlin-Marzahn and Salzburg-Maxglan internment camps who were subsequently deported to concentration camps.

Discriminatory Compensation Law
Until its revision in 1965, the post-war Federal Compensation Law excluded financial compensation for the majority of

4   ibid.

Sinti and Roma Holocaust survivors. In February 1950, the Baden-Württemberg Ministry of the Interior circulated a directive for verifying applications for financial compensation submitted by survivors of Nazi persecution and incarceration in concentration camps. It read:

> The investigation into the eligibility of Gypsies and Gypsy half-castes [Nazi jargon] for compensation, according to Federal Compensation Law, concluded that in many cases this group was not persecuted and incarcerated for racial reasons, but for its asocial and criminal behaviour. We therefore herewith decree that the applications for compensation from Gypsies and Gypsy half-castes initially be directed to the Criminal Identification Office in Stuttgart. The Stuttgart Office will carry out its investigations in co-operation with the Central Office for Criminal Investigation and Police Statistics in Munich and with the Police Authority for Vagrants in Karlsruhe.

The Federal High Court's (BGH) judgement on 7 January 1956 regarding compensation adopted the approach of the Baden-Württemberg Ministry of the Interior and consequently deportations carried out prior to March 1943 were judged to be "resettlement". Years of incarceration in concentration camps such as Belzec, Krychow and Siedlce, where thousands of Sinti and Roma died, were judged to have been a preventive measure stemming from interests of national security. More than ten years after the war the same racist views dominated the grounds for verification of compensation. In 1956, the Supreme Court opined: "Gypsies tend toward crime, especially theft and fraud. They totally lack the moral instinct to respect the property of others, because, as primitive people, they are governed by unrestrained dominating instinct." This racist statement concurred with the Nazi perception of 'Zigeuner criminality' as being a genetically transmitted and incurable disease.

Dr Kurt May, head of the Central Office of the United Restitution Organisation (URO) in Frankfurt, was one of the few people in the FRG who worked to revise the Supreme

Court's decision. He encouraged Hans Buchheim, a historian at the Institute for Contemporary History (IfZ) in Munich, to investigate the May 1940 Gypsy deportation to Poland. He also encouraged Franz Calvelli-Adorno, President of the Senate of the District Court in Frankfurt, to publish a criticism of the Supreme Court's verdict. Calvelli-Adorno wrote:

> The injustice done to Gypsies must be defined as racial persecution. The individual Gypsy was treated as asocial only because he belonged to the Gypsy race. Membership was enough to differentiate him from the rest of the population and to subordinate him, without investigation, to illegal and cruel treatment.[5]

The Federal Supreme Court judgement of 7 January 1956 was revised seven years later. The racial persecution of the Sinti and Roma was now recognised as having begun with the Campaign against the Gypsy Plague decree of 8 December 1938. The Federal Compensation Law of 1965 confirmed this position. Nevertheless, applications for compensation for internment in the internment camps in Berlin-Marzahn, Dieselstraße in Frankfurt, and Lackenbach in Burgenland, Austria, prior to deportation to the concentration camps were rejected. Likewise, claims for compensation submitted on the grounds of forced sterilisation and 'medical experiments' undertaken after 1943 were rejected, the former with reference to 'assent', even when this was given under threat of internment in a concentration camp, or when internees were promised release, the latter because an injury to health affecting earning capacity could not be substantiated. Moreover, forced sterilisation prior to 1943 was not judged to have been the result of Nazi persecution.

The 1965 law also permitted new hearing proceedings regarding applications for compensation that had been denied for persecution between 1938 and 1943. The initial one-year period prescribed for reapplication was extended to 1969.

5   Gilad Margalit, *Germany and its Gypsies. A Post-Auschwitz Ordeal*. Madison 2002.

However, many victims of Nazi persecution had in the mean-time died or, in resignation, abandoned their battle with the courts after being once again exposed to institutional racial discrimination by public authorities. Application for compensation was not made easy with application forms formulated in incomprehensible legalese and, when essential personal documents were officially deemed to have been mislaid or destroyed in the war. Following protests by Sinti and Roma Civil Rights activists, files resurfaced in the 1980s and 1990s indicating that they had been intentionally made inaccessible to the survivors.

Compensation claims for the physical or psychological after-effects of concentration camp incarceration were almost invariably rejected. Most survivors lacked the financial resources to employ a private doctor to oppose the official Compensation Office doctors' report. When occasionally such a private doctor's report was submitted the application was generally rejected on the grounds that no connection could be established between the illness which appeared, for example, a year after liberation, and the incarceration in concentration camps.

Disadvantages due to prohibited school attendance or apprenticeship were not acknowledged. Appropriated property, valuables or businesses were rarely compensated.

In 1966, the Federal High Court judged the May 1940 deportations to Poland to the ghettos of Lodz, Warsaw, Krakow, etc. and to the concentration camps of Belzec, Krychow, Siedlce and others to have been racial persecution. However, entitlement to compensation was only accepted when the applicant could substantiate that the living conditions in Poland had been the equivalent of imprisonment.

When, after a long battle with the authorities, and then mostly only with the aid of legal counsel, a claim was finally recognised, often no payment of compensation was received because other state benefits such as social welfare were deducted.

In August 1981, on the initiative of the Civil Rights

Movement organised by a group of Sinti and Roma activists, the Federal Government established a hardship fund (Härtefonds) from which a single benefit payment of up to 5,000 DM was allocated when elderly survivors found themselves in need and totally without any financial compensation. But when only minimal sums of compensation had been paid, for example, 124 DM as reimbursement of the "special race tax" (Rasse-Sondersteuer) on income tax, no grant was made from the hardship fund.

The years of battle with the authorities for recognition of the right of compensation were humiliating for all the surviving Sinti and Roma. Almost without exception applicants for compensation encountered distrust and disrespect, their statements being regarded with suspicion. Even Auschwitz survivors, who could show their tattooed prisoner number, invariably had to take legal action to acquire compensation. Lawyers' fees then amounted to a large part of the compensation paid. Often survivors had to request documents from the same civil servants who had taken part in their deportation.

The Sinti and Roma Civil Rights Movement
In contrast to the countless publications about the Nazi extermination of the Jews, it was almost four decades after the war before historians turned to the theme of the Nazi persecution of the Sinti and Roma. Apart from a very few isolated articles, the first publications that appeared before 1980 were Kenrick and Puxon's book *The Destiny of Europe's Gypsies* which had been published in 1972; Tilman Zülch's edited collection of articles *In Auschwitz vergast, bis heute verfolgt* (Gassed in Auschwitz, Persecuted until Today) published in 1979 – Tilman Zülch is co-founder and secretary general of the human rights organisation the Society for Threatened Peoples (Gesellschaft für bedrohte Völker [GfbV]) – and the first publications by Romani Rose, Chairman of the Central Council of German Sinti and Roma. In the mid 1980s research began to focus on the persecution of the 'forgotten

victims'. Having established that the Sinti and Roma, like the Jews, had been persecuted on racial grounds, a comparison was and continues to be made between these two groups either claiming the singularity of the Jewish Shoah or emphasising the differences in the racial persecution of the two groups whereby, even when not intended, the Sinti and Roma are often marginalised and effectively defined as second-class victims.

After liberation the two largest groups of former concentration camp prisoners, the Jews and political prisoners, established aid organisations for their members. Before establishing their own organisations the Sinti and Roma received assistance from the aid organisation of former political prisoners, the Organisation of Victims of the Nazi Regime (Vereinigung der Verfolgten des Naziregimes [VVN]).

A Sinti and Roma civil rights movement emerged at the end of the 1970s through a partnership between activists of the Association of German Sinti (Verband Deutscher Sinti) in Heidelberg and the Society for Endangered Peoples (Gesellschaft für bedrohte Völker) in Göttingen. The Central Council of German Sinti and Roma (Zentralrat Deutscher Sinti und Roma), modelled on the Central Council of Jews in Germany (Zentralrat der Juden in Deutschland), was founded by eleven associations of federal states (Landesverbänden) and regional associations of German Sinti and Roma in Heidelberg in February 1982. Its work focused on informing the public about the Nazi persecution and genocide, the prosecution of perpetrators, the payment of compensation to survivors, assistance to families with social problems and in dealings with public authorities, the fight against discrimination, especially in the media, and against police harassment of German Sinti and Roma. Romani Rose, whose family were victims of Nazi persecution and who together with Porrajmos survivors and other members of the post-war generation of Sinti and Roma established the civil rights movement, is chairman of the Council.

Public protests and actions such as the international commemorative meeting in the former Bergen-Belsen concentration camp on 27 October 1979, at which Simone Weil, President of the European Parliament (1979–82) and Jewish survivor of Auschwitz and Bergen-Belsen, gave the commemorative speech, and the hunger strike in the former Dachau concentration camp at Easter 1980 brought attention to the fate of the Sinti and Roma, especially the decades of denial of the Nazi genocide and continuing racial discrimination. The Third Roma World Congress, held in Göttingen 16–20 May 1981 under the leadership of Romani Rose, reached agreement between German Sinti and Roma regarding common political demands and future co-operation. The Documentary and Cultural Centre was opened in Heidelberg in 1987 and has helped to fight prejudice and inform about the life and culture of German Sinti and Roma.

Seven years after the founding of the Central Council in 1982 the socialist government (SPD) of the time, under the leadership of Chancellor Helmut Schmidt, granted political recognition in the German Bundestag (Lower House of the German Parliament) of the racial persecution and genocide of the Sinti and Roma, with the support of the Helmut Kohl led opposition party (CDU). The work of the Civil Rights Movement led to a gradual change in the perception and treatment of Sinti and Roma. Members of this national minority began to receive more respect and regard from public authorities, church institutions, Holocaust memorial sites, the regional centres for political education (Landeszentralen für politische Bildung) and the public at large. Significant progress was made when the around 60,000 German Sinti and Roma (circa 0.1 per cent of the German population) were recognised as a national minority when in May 1995 Germany signed the EU Convention for the Protection of National Minorities in the Council of Europe in Strasbourg. Germany explicitly included the German Sinti and Roma. This convention was supplemented by the European

Charter for Regional or Minority Languages. Romani, the language of the Sinti and Roma, is now awarded special protection.

From the mid 1980s Roma not aligned with the Central Council began to organise themselves independently of the Central Council. In particular, the Rom Union Frankfurt, the Rom e.V. in Cologne and the Rom and Cinti Union in Hamburg began to form a refugee-support movement and to fight for the right of settlement in Germany for Roma refugees from Eastern Europe. These Roma associations developed their own strategies of action and protest, for example, in February 1989 the Rudko Kawczynski-led Rom and Cinti Union in Hamburg organised a hunger-strike at the site of the former Neuengamme concentration camp and a seven-week protest refugee camp at this site in the summer of the same year. Roma from Romania and Bulgaria took part in a four-week march through the Ruhr district in January 1990. In November 1990, EUROM, the European Rom Parliament, a concept that emerged from the realisation of opportunities for European representation through the Council of Europe and the EU, was founded at a congress in Mülheim an der Ruhr. In the 1990s, with the emergence of pan-European Roma nationalism, ideological differences widened between the Central Council and the Roma and Cinti Union in Hamburg, which in 1994 added the title Roma National Congress (RNC) to its name. The Central Council is concerned with national ethnic minority status while the Roma National Congress with the national status of Roma in Europe.[6]

The German Forced Labour Compensation Programme
A lack of a sense of sensitivity towards the Sinti and Roma was to be witnessed almost sixty years after the Nazi persecu-

6   Yaron Matras, The Development of the Romani Civil Rights Movement in Germany 1945–1996. In: Susan Tebbutt (ed.), *Sinti and Roma. Gypsies in German-Speaking Society and Literature*. New York and Oxford 1998.

tion regarding the German Forced Labour Compensation Programme (GFLCP), i.e. compensation payment to former slave-labour (concentration camp survivors) and forced labour (those abducted from their homeland to work as forced labour in the German Reich). In the mid and late 1990s the New York City attorney Edward D. Fagan aggressively fought a number of class action lawsuits, on behalf of Holocaust victims, against the governments, banks, insurance companies and industry of Austria, Germany and Switzerland. His successes were probably directly responsible for the German Foundation Act being passed on 12 August 2000 and the Swiss Banks' Holocaust Victim Assets Litigation being approved by the United States District Court on 9 August 2000. The foundation, Remembrance, Responsibility and Future, initiated by German industry, commissioned various partner organisations to process the claims for compensation.

The Jewish concentration camp survivors' claims for compensation were processed by the Conference on Jewish Material Claims against Germany founded by twenty-three national and international Jewish organisations with experience of processing claims for financial compensation. The partner organisation commissioned to process the compensation claims of the Sinti and Roma concentration camp survivors was not its own organization, i.e. the Central Council of German Sinti and Roma, or a newly founded agency with the appropriate administrative and financial resources, but was the International Organisation for Migration (IOM) whose task it became to identify and indemnify all former non-Jewish forced and slave labour not living in the Czech Republic, Poland, the Russian Federation, or a country that was a republic of the former Soviet Union.

The choice of this organisation is regrettable due to both its history of precursor organisations, particularly the 1938 founded International Committee on Political Refugees (Intergovernmental Committee [IGC]) which, as the organ of the Evian Conference countries, was partial to the nonaccommodation of German and Austrian Jews seeking asylum from Nazi persecution, and the Provincial Committee for the Movement of Migrants from Europe (PICMME) founded in 1951 which was committed to regulating migration in accordance with the economic and political demands of its member countries. Today the IOM continues in this tradition which, in the case of Germany, has meant the "assisted voluntary return" of Kosovo refugees, negatively affecting Roma and Sinti. It is also regrettable that its title and work allude to the old stereotype of Sinti and Roma as being homeless nomads and not domiciled national minorities.

In addition, the IOM's centralised (Geneva, Switzerland), non-transparent, painfully slow processing of claims led to the aged surviving Sinti and Roma, who suffered Auschwitz and other concentration camps, being yet again placed at a disadvantage in comparison with other victims of Nazi racial persecution. The processing of the claims followed no comprehensible criteria. For the survivors this was reminiscent of the time of their persecution when they were likewise exposed to the caprice of the authorities. The deadline of 31 December 2001 for filing claims for compensation denied those not informed in time of their rightful compensation.

The Sinti and Roma Holocaust Memorial in Berlin
It is regrettable that at the end of the 1980s the Bürgerinitiative Perspektive Berlin (Action Group Perspective Berlin) led by Lea Rosh successfully argued for a Holocaust Memorial for Jewish victims alone in opposition to a memorial common to all victims of the Holocaust. Construction of American architect Peter Eisenmann's design for a Jewish memorial began in 2003. This decision continues the unfortunate classification and differentiated evaluation of Holocaust victims. The Jewish community contributed to the ongoing debate when at the beginning of 2004 Julius Schoeps, vice chairman of the Berlin Jewish community, argued for a

rededication of the memorial to include all victims of Nazi terror. Although in mid 2001, after years of opposition, the coalition of SPD and Green Party alliance agreed to the construction of a Holocaust Memorial for the murdered Sinti and Roma in Berlin, between the Reichstag (Parliament) and the Brandenburg Gate, a date for construction has yet to be set. A further setback occurred in November 2003 when Dr Christina Weiss, Minister of Culture, reopened the historical debate regarding the Nazi genocide of the Sinti and Roma in opposition to the Central Council of German Sinti and Roma's desire to have a quotation from former German President Roman Herzog inscribed on their monument.

Since 1996, 27 January (Auschwitz was liberated on 27 January 1945) has officially become Remembrance Day for the Victims of National Socialism when a prominent guest speaker is invited to address the Bundestag (Lower House of Parliament). Although all victims of Nazi persecution are commemorated, Jewish victims are given prominence. It is, however, generally unknown that since 1994 on 16 December (marking Himmler's Auschwitz Decree of 16 December 1942) the prevailing President of the Bundesrat (Upper House of Parliament − Federal Parliament) gives a speech in remembrance of the deportation of the Sinti and Roma to Auschwitz-Birkenau following Himmler's decree.

German Sinti and Roma today
There are three main groups of Sinti and Roma in Germany today. There are about 60,000 Sinti and Roma of German nationality. This group comprises Sinti who settled in Germany 600 years ago and Roma, mainly from Hungary, who settled in the Ruhr area and Westphalia between eighty and 150 years ago. The second group comprises East European Roma who came to West Germany at the beginning of the 1970s seeking employment. The third group comprises East European Roma refugees who arrived in the late 1980s following the collapse of communism. They came mainly from

Romania and Yugoslavia after it had disintegrated into civil war.[7]

The achievements made by and on behalf of the Sinti and Roma should not obscure the fact that within wide circles of German society prejudice and stereotypical images continue to exist and that members of this national minority are repeatedly victims of covert or overt discrimination in the media, at school, in apprenticeship, at work and socially. Even today the majority of the German population is unaware that, like the Jews, Nazi racial ideology was the cause of the persecution, deportation and genocide of the Sinti and Roma. The hierarchical evaluation and positioning of the different communities of Holocaust victims, directly or indirectly, by academics and even by those likewise persecuted by the Nazis, is not only painful for the Sinti and Roma but perpetuates, even when unintentionally, the racial basis of their persecution. And, as long as a German County Court, as in 1996, could declare that: "It is unreasonable to expect landlords to accept Gypsies as tenants, because traditionally they are predominantly nomadic" there is much mutual educational work to be done.

Sinti and Roma live on the fringes of German society. Antipathy toward Sinti and Roma is stronger than toward any other ethnic group, anti-Gypsyism being deeply ingrained in the majority German population. The long-term after-effects of Nazi persecution on the survivors and their descendants together with the experience of continued rejection and discrimination have only deepened Sinti mistrust of the majority population. Post-war local authority policy has effectively excluded Sinti and Roma from social contact with the majority society, resulting in an inequality of social and economic opportunity. Although the number of Sinti and Roma with school qualifications has increased, the increasingly competitive labour

---

7   Susan Tebbutt, Sinti and Roma: From Scapegoats and Stereotypes to Self-
     Assertion. In: Susan Tebbutt (ed.), *Sinti and Roma. Gypsies in German-Speaking
     Society and Literature*. New York and Oxford 1998.

market has meant that job qualification requirements have risen faster. Traditional Sinti and Roma occupations such as dealing in scrap metal, the restoration of antiques or making musical instruments are today barely economically sustaining.[8] It is regrettable that after centuries of discrimination and persecution of the German Sinti and Roma, specifically after the Nazi genocide, Germany, despite its democratisation and critical confrontation with its Nazi past, has not succeeded in providing equality of opportunity for this minority.

8   Peter Widmann, Das Erbe des Ausschlusses. Sinti und Jenische in der kommunalen Minderheitenpolitik Nachkriegsdeutschlands. In: Yaron Matras/Hans Winterberg/Michael Zimmermann (eds.), *Sinti, Roma, Gypsies. Sprache – Geschichte – Gegenwart*. Berlin 2003.

Glossary

Sinti
Feminine singular *Sintezza*, masculine singular *Sinto*.
The Sinti are principally the Roma group resident in German-speaking lands. The German term, Sinti and Roma, is specific to the Roma population in Germany where the Sinti form the majority. The German Sinti are closely related culturally with the Manush in Alsace, France, and the Sinti in Styria, Austria, northern Italy, the Netherlands and Belgium.

Roma
Feminine singular *Romni*, masculine singular *Rom*.
Rom literally means man. Outside German-speaking lands in Europe it is the collective term for all Roma groups including the Sinti. Specifically in Austria and Germany it is the term for Roma from eastern and southern Europe.

Romani chib
Romani chib is the language of the Roma. The language belongs to the Indic branch of the Indo-European languages with borrowings from Persian, Armenian and Greek. Today the numerous dialects incorporate extensive borrowings from local European languages. Most of its speakers are bilingual. The language is probably extinct in Britain. It is an oral language but there is an increasing tendency to write in Romani. There is a desire to unify the language.

Gadze, singular *Gadzo*

Gadze is the name used by Roma to describe non-Roma.

The following names are those given to the Roma by outsiders and have racial, derogatory and discriminatory connotations.

Gypsies

Gypsy is a corruption of *Egyptian,* a name by which the Roma were known in several countries from the medieval period onwards.

Gypsy in English, Gitan in French and Gitano in Spanish are all derivations of *Egyptian.*

Zigeuner

The Byzantines commonly referred to the Roma by the Greek term Atsinganoi. Atsinganoi is possibly a corruption of Athinganoi. The Athinganoi were a heretical sect. The names Atsiganos in Greek, Cingene in Turkish, Tsigan in Bulgarian, Tigan in Romanian, Ciganyok in Hungarian, Cygan in Polish, Tsiganes in French, Zingari in Italian and Zigeuner in German are all derived from Athinganoi.

The majority of German Sinti and Roma reject the term Zigeuner.

Select Bibliography

1. Introductory and General Literature

Benz, Wolfgang/ Grami, Hermann/ Weiß, Hermann (eds.). *Enzyklopädie des Nationalsozialismus*. Stuttgart: Klett-Cotta, 1998.

Burleigh, Michael/ Wippermann, Wolfgang; *The Racial State: Germany 1933–1945*. New York: Cambridge University Press, 1991.

Crow, David/ Koistin, John, *The Gypsies of Eastern Europe*. Armonk, N.Y.: M.E. Sharpe, 1991.

Fings, Karola, Heuss, Herbert and Sparing, Frank, *The Gypsies during the Second World War*. Volume 1: From Race Science to the Camps. Hatfield, Hertfordshire: University of Hertfordshire Press, 1997.

Fraser, Angus, *The Gypsies*. Oxford, UK; Cambridge, USA: Blackwell, 1995.

Friedlander, Henry, *The Origins of Nazi Genocide. From Euthenasia to The Final Solution*. Chapel Hill: University of North Carolina Press, 1997.

Giere, Jacqueline (ed.), *Die gesellschaftliche Konstruktion des Zigeuners. Zur Genese eines Vorurteils*. Frankfurt am Main; New York: Campus, 1996.

Hancock, Ian, *We are the Romani People*. Hatfield, Hertfordshire: University of Hertfordshire Press, 2002.

Hehemann, Rainer, *Die "Bekämpfung des Zigeunerunwesens" im Wilhelminischen Deutschland und in der Weimarer Republik, 1871–1933*. Frankfurt am Main: Haag + Herchen, 1987.

Hund, Wulf D. (ed.), *Zigeuner. Geschichte und Struktur einer rassistischen Konstruktion*. Duisburg: DISS, 1996.

Kenrick, Donald (Ed), *The Gypsies during the Second World war*. Volume 2: In the shadow of the Swastika. Hatfield: 1999

Kenrick, Donald/ Puxon, Grattan, *Gypsies under the Swastika*. Hatfield: 1995.

Kenrick, Donald/ Puxon, Grattan, *The Destiny of Europe's Gypsies*. New York: Basic Books, 1972.

Select Bibliography

Klamper, Elisabeth, Persecution and Annihilation of Roma and Sinti in Austria, 1938–1945. In: *Journal of the Gypsy Lore Society* 5, Vol. 3, No. 2, 1993, pp. 55-65.

Krausnick, Michail, *Wo sind die hingekommen? Der unterschlagene Völkermord an den Sinti und Roma*. Gerlingen: Bleicher, 1995.

Liégeois, Jean-Pierre, *Gypsies. An Illustrated History*. London: Al Saqi Books, 1986.

Lucassen, Leo, Zigeuner. *Die Geschichte eines polizeilichen Ordnungsbegriffs in Deutschland. 1700-1945*. Weimar: Böhlau, 1996.

Milton, Sybil, Nazi Policies toward Roma and Sinti, 1933-1945. *Journal of the Gypsy Lore Society* 5(2), pp. 1-18.

Mitscherlich, Alexander/Mielke, Fred (eds.), *The Death Doctors*. London: Elek Books, 1962.

Müller-Hill, Benno, *Murderous Science: Elimination by Scientific Selection of Jews, Gypsies, and Others in Germany, 1933-1945*. New York: Oxford University Press, 1988.

Niedersächsischen Verband Deutscher Sinti e.V. (ed.), "Es war unmenschmöglich". *Sinti aus Niedersachsen erzählen. Verfolgung und Vernichtung im Nationalsozialismus und Diskriminierung bis heute*. Hannover: Niedersächsischer Verband Deutscher Sinti, 1995.

Reemstsma, Katrin, *Sinti und Roma: Geschichte, Kultur, Gegenwart*. Munich: C.H. Beck, 1996.

Reichert, Hansjörg, Im Gleichschritt ... Sinti und Roma in Feldgrau. In: *Militärgeschichtliche Mitteilungen* 53 (1994), Booklet 2, pp. 377-397.

Riechert, Hansjörg, *Im Schatten von Auschwitz. Die nationalsozialistische Sterilisationspolitik gegenüber Sinti und Roma*. Münster; New York: Waxmann, 1995.

Rigg, Bryan Mark, *Hitler's Jewish Soldiers. The Untold Story of Nazi Racial Laws and Men of Jewish Descent in the German Military*. Lawrence, Kansas: University Press of Kansas, 2002.

Rose, Romani (ed.), "Den Rauch hatten wir täglich vor Augen". *Der nationalsozialistische Völkermord an den Sinti und Roma. Heidelberg: Dokumentations- und Kulturzentrum Deutscher Sinti und Roma, 1999*. (Catalogue of the permanent exhibition in the Documentation and Cultural Centre of German Sinti and Roma, Heidelberg).

Rose, Romani (ed.), *The National Socialist Genocide of the Sinti and Roma. Heidelberg: Documentation and Cultural Centre German Sinti and Roma*, 2003. (Catalogue of the permanent exhibition in the State Museum Auschwitz).

Tebbutt, Susan, *Sinti and Roma in German-speaking Society and Literature*. New York: Berghahn Books, 1998.

Tyrnauer, Gabrielle, *Gypsies and the Holocaust: A Bibliographical and Intro-ductory Essay*. Montreal: Montreal Institute for Genocide Studies, 1991.

Wistrich, Robert, *Who's who in Nazi Germany*. London; New York: Routledge, 1995.

Zimmermann, Michael, *Rassenutopie und Genozid. Die nationalsozialis-tische "Lösung der Zigeunerfrage"*. Hamburg: Christians, 1996.

2. *Auschwitz-Birkenau, Ravensbrück, Sachsenhausen, SS-Brigade "Dirlewanger"*

Adelsberger, Lucie, Auschwitz. *Ein Tatsachenbericht. Das Vermächtnis der Opfer für uns Juden und für alle Menschen*. Berlin: Lettner-Verlag, 1956.

Adler, Hans Günter/Langbein, Hermann/Lingens-Reiner, Ella (eds.), *Auschwitz. Zeugnisse und Berichte*. Frankfurt am Main: Athenäum, 1988.

Arndt, Ino, Das Frauenkonzentrationslager Ravensbrück. In: *Studien zur Geschichte der Konzentrationslager. Schriftenreihe der Vierteljahreshefte für Zeitgeschichte 21*. Martin Brozat (ed.). Stuttgart, 1970. pp. 93-129.

Auerbach, Helmuth, Die Einheit Dirlewanger. In: *Vierteljahresheft für Zeitgeschichte 10* (1962), Booklet 2. pp. 250-263.

Broad, Pery, KZ Auschwitz. Reminiscences of Pery Broad, SS-man in the Auschwitz concentration camp. In: *Hefte von Auschwitz 9*. 1966. pp. 7-48.

Czech, Danuta, *Auschwitz Chronicle, 1939-1945*. New York: Henry Holt, 1990.

Heuzeroth, Günter/Martinß, Karl-Heinz, Vom Ziegelhof nach Auschwitz. Verfolgung und Vernichtung der Sinti und Roma. In *Heuzeroth, Günter, Unter der Gewaltherrschaft des Nationalsozialismus 1933-1945*. Dargestellt an den Ereignissen im Oldenburger Land. Vol. 2 Verfolgte aus rassischen Gründen. Oldenburg: Universität Oldenburg, Zentrum für pädagogische Berufspraxis, 1985.

Höß, Rudolf, *Commandant in Auschwitz. Autobiography of Rudolf Höß*. Martin Broszat (ed.). Cleveland: World Publishing Company, 1960.

Klausch, Hans-Peter, *Antifaschisten in SS-Uniform. Schicksal und Wider-stand der deutschen politischen KZ-Häftlinge, Zuchthaus- und Wehrmachtsstrafgefangenen in der SS-Sonderformation Dirlewanger*. Bremen: Edition Temmen, 1993.

Kühn, Rainer, *Konzentrationslager Sachsenhausen*. Berlin: Die Landeszen-trale, 1990.

Langbein, Hermann, *Der Auschwitz-Prozess. Eine Dokumentation*. 2 Vol-

Select Bibliography

umes. Frankfurt am Main: Neue Kritik, 1995.

Langbein, Hermann, Im Zigeunerlager von Auschwitz. In: Zülch, Tilman (ed.), In Auschwitz vergast, bis heute verfolgt. Zur Situation der Roma (Zigeuner) in Deutschland und Europa. Reinbek: Rowohlt, 1983. pp. 134-135.

Langbein, Hermann, People in Auschwitz. Chapel Hill, NC: University of North Carolina Press, 2004.

MacLean, French L., The Cruel Hunters: SS-Sonderkommando Dirlewanger, Hitler's Most Notorious Anti-Partisan Unit. Atglen, PA: Schiffer Pub. 1998.

Memorial Book. The Gypsies at Auschwitz-Birkenau. Volumes I and II. Edited by the State Museum of Auschwitz in co-operation with the Documentary and Cultural Centre of German Sinti and Roma, Heidelberg. Editorial Director: Jan Parcer. Preface by Romani Rose. Munich/London/New York/Paris: K.G. Saur, 1993.

Michalak, Wanda (ed.), Auschwitz. Geschichte und Wirklichkeit eines Vernichtungslagers. Reinbek: Rowohlt, 1982.

Müller, Filip, Eyewitness Auschwitz: three years in the gas chambers. Chicago: Ivan R. Dee, 1999.

Rüdiger, Gerhard F., "Jeder Stein ein Blutstropfen". Zigeuner in Auschwitz-Birkenau, Oswiecim-Brzezinka. In: Zülch, Tilman (ed.), In Auschwitz vergast, ... Reinbek: Rowohlt, 1983. pp. 135-146.

Sandner, Peter, Frankfurt. Auschwitz. Die nationalsozialistische Verfolgung der Sinti und Roma in Frankfurt am Main. Frankfurt am Main: Brandes & Apsel, 1998.

Smolen, Kazimierz, Das Schicksal der Sinti und Roma im KL Auschwitz-Birkenau. In: Verband der Roma in Polen (ed.), Los Cyganów w KL Auschwitz-Birkenau/Das Schicksal der Sinti und Roma im KL Auschwitz-Birkenau. Oswiecim, 1994. pp. 129-175.

Sonneman, Toby, Shared Sorrows. A Gypsy Family Remembers the Holocaust. Hatfield, Hertfordshire: University of Hertfordshire Press, 2002.

3. Postwar

Becker, Ingeborg/Huber, Harold/Kuester, Otto, Bundesentschädigungsgesetze (BEG). Berlin: F. Vahlen, 1955.

Calvelli-Adorno, Franz, Die rassische Verfolgung der Zigeuner vor dem 1. März 1943. In: Rechtsprechung zur Wiedergutmachung 12 (12). pp. 529-537.

Feuerhelm, Wolfgang, Polizei und "Zigeuner": Strategien, Handlungsmuster und Alltagstheorien im polizeilichen Umgang mit Sinti und Roma. Stuttgart: F. Enke, 1987.

Geigges, Anita/Wette, Bernhard, *Zigeuner heute. Verfolgung und Diskriminierung in der BRD.* Bornheim-Merten: Lamuv-Verlag, 1979.

Gilsenbach, Reimar, *O Django, sing deinen Zorn! Sinti und Roma unter den Deutschen.* Berlin: BasisDruck, 1993.

Herbst, Ludolf/Goschler, Constantin (eds.), *Wiedergutmachung in der Bundesrepublik Deutschland.* Munich: R. Oldenbourg, 1989.

Klüver, Reymer: *Gezeichnet für alle Zeiten. Süddeutsche Zeitung,* Page 3, Edition 23.6.2003.

Krokowski, Heike, *Die Last der Vergangenheit. Auswirkungen nationalsozialistischer Verfolgung auf deutsche Sinti.* Frankfurt am Main; New York: Campus, 2001.

Margalit, Gilad, *Germany and its Gypsies. A Post-Auschwitz Ordeal.* Madison, Wisconsin: University of Wisconsin Press, 2002.

Pross, Christian, *Paying for the Past: The Struggle over Reparations for Surviving Victims of the Nazi Terror.* Baltimore: John Hopkins, 1998.

Rose, Romani, *Bürgerrechte für Sinti und Roma. Das Buch zum Rassismus in Deutschland.* Heidelberg: Dokumentations- und Kulturzentrum Deutscher Sinti und Roma, 1987.

Rose, Romani, *Wir wollen Bürgerrechte und keinen Rassismus.* Heidelberg: Dokumentations- und Kulturzentrum Deutscher Sinti und Roma, 1987.

Widmann, Peter, Das Erbe des Ausschlusses. Sinti und Jenische in der kommunalen Minderheitenpolitik Nachkriegsdeutschlands. In: Matras, Yaron/Winterberg, Hans/Wippermannn, Michael (Eds.), *Sinti, Roma, Gypsies. Sprache – Geschichte – Gegenwart.* Berlin: Metropol, 2003.

Wippermann, Wolfgang, Christine Lehmann and Mazurka Rose. Two Gypsies in the Grip of German Bureaucracy. In: Burleigh, Michael (eds.), *Confronting the Nazi Past. New Debates on Modern German History.* New York: St. Martin's Press, 1996. pp. 112-124.

Wippermann, Wolfgang, "Wider die Gutmachung". Die versagte Wiedergutmachung an den Sinti und Roma. In: *Nes Ammin, Zeichen für die Völker* 1 / 1997. pp. 3-12.

Zentralrat Deutscher Sinti und Roma (ed.), Minderheitenschutz für Sinti und Roma in Rahmen des Europarates, der KSZE und der UNO. Heidelberg: Zentralrat Deutscher Sinti und Roma, 1994.

Zülch, Tilman (ed.), *In Auschwitz vergast, bis heute verfolgt. Zur Situation der Roma (Zigeuner) in Deutschland und Europa.* Reinbek: Rowohlt, 1983.

4. Biographies

Hackl, Erich, *Farewell Sidonia*. New York: Fromm International Publishing, 1992.

Rosenberg, Otto, *A Gypsy in Auschwitz*. London: London House, 1999.

5. Documentary Films

Case, George (Director), *The Forgotten Holocaust: The Persecution of Gypsies by the Nazis. BBC1 Inside Story. UK 1989*. (Features Eric and Walter Winter and other Sinti and Roma survivors of Auschwitz).

Abbreviations used

AGKBZH	Archiwum Głównej Komisji Bradania Zbrodni Hitlerowskich w Polsce = Archives of the Central Commission for Investigation of German Crimes in Poland
APMO	Archiwum Panstwowego Muzeum e Oswiecimiu = Archive of the State Museum Auschwitz
BAK	Bundesarchiv Koblenz = Federal Archive Koblenz
BEG	Bundesentschädigungsgesetze = Federal Compensation Law
BGH	Bundesgerichthof = Federal High Court
CDU	Christian Social Union
DFG	Deutsche Forschungsgemeinschaft = German Research Council
FRG	Federal Republic of Germany
Gestapo	Geheime Staatspolizei
GfbV	Gesellschaft für bedrohte Völker = Society for Threatened Peoples
GFLCP	German Forced Labour Compensation Programme
IfZ	Institut für Zeitgeschichte = Institute of Contemporary History
IG	Interessengemeinschaft = Combine (IG Farben)
IOM	International Organisation for Migration
Kapo	Kameradschaftspolizei. Prisoners appointed by the SS to be in charge of a work detail. Infamous for their brutality.
KL	Konzentrationslager = concentration camp
Kripo	Kriminalpolizei = Criminal Police. In 1939 it became Section V of the RSHA under Arthur Nebe.

Abbrievations used

KZ	Konzentrationslager = concentration camp
ND	Nürnberger Dokumente = Nuremberg Document
NSDAP	Nationalsozialistische Deutsche Arbeiterpartei = National Socialist German Workers Party – Nazi Party
RAD	Reichsarbeitsdienst = German Labour Service
RHF	Rassenhygienische Forschungsstelle = Research Centre for Racial Hygiene and Population Biology
RKPA	Reichskriminalpolizeiamt = Reich Criminal Police Department
RSHA	Reichssicherheitshauptamt = Reich Security Main Office
RuSHA	Rasse- und Siedlungshauptamt = Race and Resettlement Main Office
SA	Sturmabteilung = Storm Troopers. Nazi terrorist militia, organized around 1924.
SD	Sicherheitsdienst = Security Service of the SS. The Nazi party's intelligence service; a major instrument for the implementation of the "Final Solution." Reinhard Heydrich was its head.
SPD	Social Democratic Party
SS	Schutzstaffel = protection squad. A paramilitary organization within the Nazi party that provided Hitler's bodyguard, security forces including the Gestapo, concentration camp guards, and a corps of combat troops (the Waffen SS).
STA	Staatsarchiv = State Archives
URO	United Restitution Organisation
VVN	Vereinigung der Verfolgten des Naziregimes = Organisation of the Victims of Nazism
WVHA	Wirtschafts-Verwaltungshauptamt der SS = Economic–Administrative Main Office, the central administration for SS economic activities based in Berlin. Amtsgruppe (Branch) II D was the inspectorate of concentration camps. This office, headed by SS-Standartenführer Gerhard Maurer, negotiated contracts with industrial firms for the use of concentration camp prisoners – numbers, type of work, food and accommodation, and financial compensation per prisoner per day.